GET OUT
THE VOTE!

GET OUT

HOW TO INCREASE VOTER TURNOUT

THE VOTE!

Donald P. Green

Alan S. Gerber

Brookings Institution Press
Washington, D.C.

Copyright © 2004
THE BROOKINGS INSTITUTION
1775 Massachusetts Avenue, N.W., Washington, D.C. 20036
www.brookings.edu

Library of Congress Cataloging-in-Publication data

Green, Donald P., 1961–
Get out the vote : how to increase voter turnout /
Donald P. Green, Alan S. Gerber.
   p.   cm.
Includes bibliographical references and index.
   ISBN 0-8157-3268-6 (cloth : alk. paper)
   ISBN 0-8157-3269-4 (pbk. : alk. paper)
   1. Political campaigns—United States. 2. Campaign management—
United States. 3. Voting—United States. I. Gerber, Alan S. II. Title.
   JK2281.G74   2004
   324.7'0973—dc22   2004000391

9 8 7 6 5 4 3

The paper used in this publication meets minimum requirements of the
American National Standard for Information Sciences—Permanence of Paper
for Printed Library Materials: ANSI Z39.48-1992.

Typeset in Life and Univers Condensed

Composition by Cynthia Stock
Silver Spring, Maryland

Printed by R. R. Donnelley
Harrisonburg, Virginia

Contents

Preface

What are the most cost-effective ways to increase voter turnout? Whether the ambition is to win elections, promote civic engagement in a community, or bolster the legitimacy of democratic institutions, this question is of enormous practical significance. To date, however, discussions of how best to mobilize voters have been rather unsystematic and short on reliable evidence. Most books on campaign strategy mention the importance of mobilizing voters but focus primarily on how to persuade voters. Training guides for nonpartisan groups tend to walk through a variety of get-out-the-vote techniques without marshaling any evidence about their effectiveness.

This book presents a practical guide to managing get-out-the-vote drives, while at the same time pulling together all of the scientific evidence about the cost-effectiveness of face-to-face canvassing, leafleting, direct mail, phone calls, and electronic mail. Following our initial field experiment in New Haven in 1998, which compared the effects of nonpartisan, face-to-face canvassing, phone calls, and mailings, our research took many directions. Alan Gerber took the lead in extending the research to consider the effects of campaign activity in partisan contests. Don Green concentrated on broadening the work to interest group activity and a wider array of nonpartisan phone and canvassing appeals. These efforts were complemented by those of other scholars, who performed additional studies. Five election years over the period 1998–2002 have furnished a wealth of studies that encompass municipal, state, and federal contests; campaigns run by Democrats, Republicans, interest groups, and nonpartisan coalitions; campaigns targeting populations living in urban, rural, and suburban neighborhoods; and voter mobilization efforts directed at African Americans, Latinos, and Asian Americans. Although many questions remain unanswered, these studies have brought new scientific rigor to the study of campaigns. Unfortunately, most have been published in technical, academic journals. This book aims to bring this research to the attention of a broader audience.

We are deeply indebted to the many researchers, candidates, consultants, organizations, and campaign workers who made this line of research possible. Most of the studies reported here were conducted under our direction, but their execution depended on a talented pool of Yale doctoral students. David Nickerson supervised the Youth Vote experiments in 2000 and 2002, the Votes For Students experiments in 2002, and the Michigan Democrats experiment in 2002. Our thanks go also to Andra Gillespie, Matthew Green, Christopher Mann, Barry McMillion, John Phillips, and Jennifer Smith, who assisted in a variety of experiments and whose original research contributed immensely to this book. Kevin Arceneaux, Sandy Newman, and Jennifer Smith read early drafts of this manuscript and offered many useful suggestions.

We are indebted as well to researchers from other universities, who graciously shared their results with us: Elizabeth Bennion (University of Indiana, South Bend), Ryan Friedrichs and David King (Harvard), John McNulty (University of California, Berkeley), Melissa Michelson (California State University, Fresno), and Ricardo Ramírez and Janelle Wong (University of Southern California).

Special thanks go to the campaigns and organizations that allowed us to study their voter mobilization efforts. Organizations such as the National Voter Fund of the National Association for the Advancement of Colored People, the Youth Vote Coalition, Votes For Students, National Association of Latino Elected Officials, and several partisan campaigns that asked to remain anonymous deserve the gratitude of all those who will learn from their experiences.

Financial support for our research has come from a variety of sources. The Smith Richardson Foundation funded our first studies in 1998. The Pew Charitable Trusts invited us to evaluate the Youth Vote campaign in 2000. A grant from the CIRCLE at the University of Maryland made possible our 2001 and 2002 studies of Youth Vote and Votes For Students. We wish to thank Mark Steinmeyer (Smith Richardson), Tobi Walker and Michael Delli Carpini (Pew), and William Galston (CIRCLE) for their support and encouragement. We are grateful as well to the Institution for Social and Policy Studies at Yale University, which provided research funding, a home for our sprawling projects, and a superb administrative staff. None of these funders, of course, bears any responsibility for the conclusions we draw.

Finally, we wish to express our gratitude to Beth Weinberger, who assembled and edited this volume. Building on the important early contributions of Christopher Mann, Rachel Milstein, David Nickerson, David Ogle, and Jennifer Smith, Beth brought the book to life in its current form.

GET OUT THE VOTE!

CHAPTER ONE

Why Voter Mobilization Matters

The United States has the busiest election calendar on earth. Thanks to the many layers of federal, state, and local government, Americans have more opportunities to vote each decade than Britons, Germans, or Japanese have in their lifetime. Thousands of Americans seek elective office each year, running for legislative, judicial, and administrative posts.

Given the frequency with which elections occur and the mundane quality of most of the contests, those who write about elections tend to focus exclusively on the high-visibility contests for president, senator, or governor. This focus gives a distorted impression of how election battles are typically waged. First, high-profile races often involve professionalized campaigns, staffed by a coterie of media consultants, pollsters, speechwriters, and event coordinators. Second, in order to reach large and geographically dispersed populations, these campaigns often place enormous emphasis on mass communications, such as television advertising. Third, the importance of these races calls press attention to the issues at stake and the attributes of the candidates.

The typical election, by contrast, tends to be waged on a smaller scale and at a more personal level. Few candidates for state representative or probate judge have access to the financial resources needed to produce and air television commercials. Even long-standing incumbents in state and municipal posts are often unknown to a majority of their constituents. The challenge that confronts candidates in low-salience elections is to target potential supporters and get them to the polls, while living within the constraints of a tight campaign budget.

A similar challenge confronts political and nonpartisan organizations that seek to mobilize voters for state and local elections. Making scarce campaign dollars go as far as possible requires those who manage these campaigns to think hard about the trade-offs. Is it best to assemble a local phone bank? Hire a telemarketing firm? Field a team of canvassers to contact voters door-to-door? Send direct mail and, if so, how many pieces of direct mail?

This book offers a guide for campaigns and organizations that seek to formulate cost-effective strategies for mobilizing voters. For each form of voter mobilization, we pose two basic questions: (1) What steps are needed to put it into place, and (2) How many votes will be produced for each dollar spent? After summarizing the "how to do it" aspects of each get-out-the-vote (GOTV) tactic, we provide an impartial, scientifically rigorous assessment of whether it has been shown to produce votes in a cost-effective manner. The chapters that follow cover the staples of state and municipal election campaigns: door-to-door canvassing, leafleting, direct mail, and phone banks. We also discuss some newer campaign tactics, such as voter mobilization through e-mail. The concluding chapter discusses other forms of GOTV activity and the research that is currently under way to evaluate their effectiveness.

Does Voter Mobilization Matter?

The sleepy quality of many state and local elections often conceals what is at stake politically. Take, for example, the 1998 Kansas State Board of Education elections that created a six-to-four conservative majority. This election featured a well-organized campaign that used personal contact with voters to mobilize hundreds of churchgoers in low-turnout Republican primaries. This victory at the polls culminated a year later in a dramatic change in policy. In August 1999, the Kansas State Board of Education voted six to four to drop evolution from science education standards, letting localities decide whether to teach creationism in addition to or instead of evolution. This move attracted national attention and renewed debates about science curricula and religious conviction. But what occurred in Kansas is a story not only about clashing ideologies but also about how campaigns work to get voters to the polls. Very few Kansans changed their mind about the merits of evolution and creationism over the course of the election campaign. What changed in 1998—

and in subsequent elections, as countermobilization campaigns caused conservatives to lose their majority—was who showed up to vote.

Although Americans often take a cynical view of state and local elections, supposing that who fills a given office makes no difference, the Kansas example is not as exceptional as it may seem. During the 1960s, the U.S. Supreme Court struck down many states' system of legislative representation as inconsistent with the principle of "one man, one vote." Prior to the Supreme Court's rulings, several states assigned equal representation to all counties, which meant that rural voters were heavily overrepresented in proportion to their share of the population. Once state legislatures were reorganized according to the "one man, one vote" principle, the share of government funds flowing to rural counties dropped dramatically.[1] Voting power matters. When groups such as conservative Christians or elderly Americans vote in large numbers, policymakers have an incentive to take their concerns seriously. By the same token, elected officials can afford to disregard groups that vote at low rates, such as southern blacks prior to the Voting Rights Act in 1965. Largely excluded from the electorate by racially biased voter registration practices, southern blacks saw their needs for schooling, transportation, and jobs go unheeded by state and local government.

The Kansas State Board of Education elections also illustrate the power of small numbers in elections where turnout is low. The ability to mobilize a few hundred supporters can prove decisive when only a few thousand votes are cast. Knowing what it takes to generate a few hundred votes in a reliable way can therefore be extremely valuable. It can be valuable not only for a specific candidate conducting the voter mobilization campaign but also for all of the candidates who share similar party labels. Mobilizing 500 Republicans to support the GOP nominee in a state assembly race furnishes votes for Republican candidates up and down the ticket.

Getting Advice on Getting Out the Vote

Campaigns vary enormously in their goals: some are partisan, some nonpartisan; some focus on name recognition, some on persuasion, and some on mobilizing their base of loyal voters. Some campaigns seek to educate citizens, some to register citizens, and some to motivate citizens. But varied as they are, campaigns have important and obvious commonalities.

As election day approaches and campaigns move into GOTV mode, their aims become quite similar and their purposes very narrow. By the week before the election, they are all homing in on one simple task—to get their people to the polls. Each campaign struggles with the same basic question: How should remaining resources be allocated in order to turn out the largest number of targeted voters?

Ask around and you will receive plenty of advice on what is the best way to mobilize voters in those final days or weeks. You may hear that it is one part mailings to three parts phone calls for an incumbent race. You may hear that, regardless of the office, it is two parts television and radio, if you can afford it, to two parts phone calls. You may even hear that, for a nonpartisan GOTV campaign, it is four parts door-to-door canvassing, but you will never be able to get enough canvassers, so it is best just to make phone calls. Almost all this advice is based on conjecture—conjecture drawn from experience perhaps, but conjecture nonetheless (see box 1-1).

What sets this book apart from the existing "how to win an election" canon is five years of rigorous scientific research. Every study reported in this book used a *randomized experimental design*, which is a research methodology that produces a reliable way to gauge effects—in this case, the effects of GOTV interventions. In a nutshell, the experiments we report divide lists of registered voters into a group that receives the intervention in question and a group that does not. After the election is over, researchers examine public records to see who voted and then tabulate the results in order to determine whether those assigned to receive the GOTV treatment voted at higher rates than those assigned to the control group. Although these field experiments still leave room for interpretation, they go a long way toward replacing speculation with evidence.

Another aspect of our work that contributes to our objectivity is that we are not in the business of selling campaign services. In the past, scanning for truth about the effectiveness of various GOTV strategies was like having to consult with salespeople about whether or not to purchase the items they are selling. Many campaign consultants have financial interests in direct mail companies, phone banks, or media consultancy services. In this book, we make a concerted effort to incorporate the results of *every* experimental study conducted since the mid-1990s, not just the ones that are congenial to a particular point of view.

Two constraints of this work must be acknowledged at the outset. First, we have not yet looked at high-profile campaigns, such as U.S. Senate races or presidential races. Although we believe that the findings

Box 1-1. Dubious Evidence

Many campaign services can be purchased from private vendors. These vendors often present evidence about the effectiveness of their products in the form of testimonials. Here is one example from the website of a leading commercial phone bank:

On June 5, Election Day in Los Angeles, at 5 p.m. EST, [our phone bank] received a telephone call from the James Hahn for Mayor campaign. Voter turnout was heavy in precincts of his opponent, and the Hahn campaign had to get out more of his voters.

In one hour, [our phone bank] had perfected a script, manipulated voter data to match phone numbers, and programmed the calls. By the time the polls closed, our firm had placed 30,000 live GOTV calls and reached 10,000 targeted voters.

James Hahn was elected mayor with almost 54 percent of the vote.

For all we know, this phone bank did a splendid job of mobilizing voters. And, in fairness, this firm does not claim credit for Hahn's 54 percent share of the vote; the fact is simply allowed to speak for itself.

When reading this type of testimonial, it is important to bear in mind that *there is no control group.* How many votes would Hahn have won had his campaign not conducted this eleventh-hour calling campaign?

It is also useful to keep things in proportion. This phone bank spoke with 10,000 voters, but Hahn won the election by a margin of 38,782 votes.

discussed here are relevant to such large-scale campaigns insofar as they rely on GOTV tactics such as phone banks or direct mail, we have yet to conduct experiments that speak directly to the effectiveness of mass media, on which these large-scale campaigns rely heavily.

Second, although they are of obvious importance, GOTV strategies are not the only factors at play in an election. When we speak of the effectiveness of GOTV techniques, we have in mind the percentage *increase* in voter turnout that can be attributed to professional phone callers or direct mail, for instance. Using the most effective get-out-the-vote strategy will not guarantee victory. All the other factors that shape the electoral fortunes of a candidate—persona, platform, party, and campaign management—are relevant as well. A spectacularly successful GOTV campaign might lift an overmatched candidate from 28 to 38 percent or a competitive candidate from 48 to 58 percent. Often, winning elections is possible only when voter mobilization strategies are combined with messages that persuade voters to vote in a particular way (see box 1-2).

GOTV Research and Larger Questions about Why People Do Not Vote

Political observers often turn to broad-gauge explanations for why so few Americans vote: alienation from public life, the lack of a proportional representation system, the failings of civic education, the geographic mobility of the population. We might call these long-term—very long-term—GOTV considerations. Many books written by academics focus exclusively on these explanations.

This book, in contrast, is concerned with GOTV considerations in the short term. We do not discuss the ways in which political participation is shaped by fundamental features of our political, social, and economic system, although we agree that structural and psychological barriers to voting are worthy of study and that large-scale reforms might well be beneficial. In the concluding chapter, we describe research that might be useful to those interested in learning more about how voter turnout relates to these broader features of society. The focus of this book is quite different. Our aim is to look closely at how GOTV campaigns are structured and to figure out how various GOTV tactics affect voter participation. This close-to-the-ground approach is designed to provide campaigns with useful information on the effectiveness of common GOTV techniques. With six weeks until an election, even the most dedicated campaign team will not be able to reshape the country's basic constitutional framework or the political culture of American society. What a campaign can do, however, is make informed choices about its GOTV plans, ensuring that its resources are being used efficiently to produce votes.

Evidence versus War Stories

Before delving into the research findings, we want to call attention to a cluster of assumptions that often hinder informed GOTV decisionmaking. One is the belief that the experts know what works: that knowledge

Box 1-2. Generating Votes:
Mobilization versus Persuasion

In order to see how GOTV fits into campaign strategy, imagine that you are a Republican candidate running for local office. There are 8,000 registered voters, and election day is approaching. The 2,000 registered Republicans favor you 80 versus 20 percent, but ordinarily only half of them vote. The remaining 6,000 people in the electorate favor your opponent 67.5 versus 32.5 percent; one-third of them can be expected to vote. So, with 800 votes from registered Republicans and 650 from the rest of the electorate, you are in danger of losing 1,450 to 1,550:

	Voters		Nonvoters	
Intent	Registered Republicans	Others	Registered Republicans	Others
Intend to vote for you	800	650	800	1,300
Intend to vote for your opponent	200	1,350	200	2,700

Thinking about how to win in this situation is really a matter of thinking about where to find at least 100 *additional* votes. All the factors that got you those 1,450 votes—your good looks, your record in office, and so forth—are important in shaping the eventual outcome of the election, but the strategic decisions from this point forward must focus on what you will do now to change the expected outcome.

A GOTV strategy aims to transform nonvoters into voters. If you can identify the 2,100 abstainers who would vote for you, try to get at least 100 of them to the polls. Voter "ID" programs use brief polls to identify these potential supporters, who will later be targeted for mobilization.

Voter ID programs require planning and money, however. A simpler approach is to focus GOTV attention solely on Republicans. Bear in mind that if you attempt to mobilize some of the 1,000 Republicans who otherwise would not vote, you will need to get at least 167 to the polls because you only gain sixty net votes for every 100 Republicans you mobilize.

Conversely, a demobilization strategy strives to transform voters into nonvoters. You could accomplish this by scaring or demoralizing some of the 1,550 people who would otherwise cast votes for your opponent.

Finally, a persuasion strategy attempts to convert some of these 1,550 voters into your supporters. Conversions rapidly close the margin of votes between you and your opponent. Just fifty successes would make the race a dead heat. It is also possible to blend persuasion and mobilization strategies, for example, by appealing to the 2,000 Republicans in ways that both mobilize and persuade them. By focusing solely on voter mobilization, this book understates the number of net votes generated by tactics that simultaneously mobilize and persuade.

is, after all, what makes them the experts. Someone with a lot of campaign experience *must* know which tactics work and which do not under assorted circumstances. On the other end of the spectrum is the idea that no one really knows what works because no one can adequately measure what works. There is no way to rerun an election using different GOTV methods, no parallel universe in which to watch the very same campaign focusing its efforts on mass mailings, then on phone banks, and then on television ads. The final assumption is that if everybody is doing it, it must be useful: 5,000 campaigners can't be wrong about prerecorded calls!

The following six chapters respond to these misguided assumptions. In short,

✔ Experts, be they consultants, seasoned campaigners, or purveyors of GOTV technology, rarely, if ever, measure effectiveness. Hal Malchow, one of the few consultants to embrace experimentation, reports that his calls for rigorous evaluation repeatedly go unheeded. Notwithstanding the large quantities of money at stake, Malchow observes that "no one really knows how much difference mail and phone GOTV programs make."[2]

✔ Experts may report speculations in the guise of "findings," but without a rigorous research design, those "findings" are suspect. Those who manage campaigns and sell campaign services have a wealth of experience in deploying campaign resources, formulating campaign messages, and supervising campaign staff. But lacking a background in research design or statistical inference, they frequently misrepresent (innocently in many cases) correlation as causation. They might claim, for instance, that a radio GOTV campaign is responsible for increasing the Latino vote in a particular media market. In support of this assertion, they might point to the lack of change in the Latino vote in a neighboring media market. Because it is difficult to know whether the two media markets are truly comparable, we find this form of proof-by-anecdote unpersuasive.

✔ There *is* an accurate way to measure the effectiveness of GOTV techniques, namely, through experimental research. Randomly assigning a set of precincts or media markets to different campaign tactics makes meaningful causal inferences possible.

✔ Lastly, our results may surprise you. Just because everybody is doing it does not necessarily mean that it works. It appears that large sums of money are routinely wasted on ineffective GOTV tactics.

We will count ourselves successful if you not only learn from the experimental results we report but also become more discerning when evaluating claims that rest on anecdotes and other nonexperimental evidence.

Preview of Our Findings

The Kansas State Board of Education election mentioned at the outset of this chapter illustrates the central finding in our studies across eighteen states and five election years: *A personal approach to mobilizing voters is generally more effective than an impersonal approach.* That is, the more personal the interaction between campaign and potential voter, the more it raises a person's chances of voting. Door-to-door canvassing by friends and neighbors is the gold-standard mobilization tactic; chatty, unhurried phone calls seem to work well, too. Automatically dialed, prerecorded GOTV phone calls, by contrast, are utterly impersonal and, evidently, wholly ineffective at getting people to vote.

Here is the trade-off confronting those who manage campaigns: the more personal the interaction, the harder it is to reproduce on a large scale. Canvassing door-to-door is therefore not the answer for every GOTV campaign. That is why we consider this book to be a "shoppers' guide." No candidate or campaign manager can look at this book and, without considering his or her own circumstances, find the answer. The key is to assess your resources, goals, and political situation and then form a judgment about what tactics will produce the most votes at the lowest cost. What we do is provide a synopsis of scientifically rigorous evidence about what has worked in other campaigns.

Structure of the Book

We begin the book by explaining why experimental evidence warrants special attention. Chapter 2 discusses the nuts and bolts of how randomized experiments are conducted and why they are better than other approaches to studying the effectiveness of GOTV tactics. Chapters 3 through 7 present our evaluations of GOTV mobilization techniques: door-to-door, leaflets, mail, phone calls, and e-mail. These chapters discuss the practical challenges of conducting these campaigns and provide a cost-benefit analysis of each GOTV tactic. Chapter 8 wraps up by discussing the state of evidence concerning other types of voter mobilization campaigns, such as civic education programs in high schools and televised public service announcements. In the interest of helping you to customize research for your own purposes, the concluding chapter also gives some pointers about how to conduct experimental studies of voter turnout. The experimental study of voter mobilization is not some special form of sorcery known only to Yale professors. Anyone can do it. We close by discussing the role that scientifically rigorous GOTV research may play in encouraging greater levels of voter participation.

CHAPTER TWO

Evidence versus Received Wisdom

It is not hard to find advice about how to run an effective get-out-the-vote campaign. *The Road to Victory 2000,* a publication of *Campaigns and Elections* magazine, proclaims, "Nothing gets out the vote like a telephone."[1] The Democratic National Committee recommends, "If your GOTV resources allow you to do only one thing, do telephones. Telephones offer the greatest coverage with the smallest expenditure of resources."[2] In a rare show of bipartisan agreement, the Republican National Committee concurs that "election day phoning can often mean the difference between victory and defeat" but also explains to its organizers that "tried and true methods of street campaigning where candidates 'press the flesh' in door-to-door activity, voter blitzes, business tours, in-home receptions, and the like are especially effective in state legislative and local campaigns."[3] A local chapter of the Green Party emphasizes a rather different GOTV strategy: "Depending on your budget, mailers are often one of the best ways to help get out the vote." More specifically it suggests, "One or two mailers are generally adequate, with the final one coming in the mail two or three days before the election."[4] The litany of advice can easily be expanded to include prerecorded messages delivered by phone (so-called robotic, or robo, calls), leafleting (lit drops), and e-mail, as well as special combinations of phone and mail that are said to have synergistic effects.

Direct mail, phone calls, prerecorded phone calls, and precinct walking all sound like good campaign tactics, and a campaign with an infinite supply of time and money would use them all. But here on planet earth,

Box 2-1. Thinking about Cost-Effectiveness

When thinking about the cost-effectiveness of a get-out-the-vote tactic, it is helpful to ask How many dollars will it take to produce one additional vote? This yardstick will help you to compare the cost-effectiveness of various types of GOTV tactics. One tactic might produce votes at a rate of $40 per vote; another, at $75 per vote.

Keep three things in mind as you read our assessments of cost-effectiveness. First, some tactics, such as leafleting, generate votes cheaply because they give a tiny nudge to vast numbers of people. If your constituency does not have vast numbers of people, these tactics might be useless to you—even if they were free! Second, the costs and benefits we report in the chapters that follow are calculated based on the experiences of particular campaigns. A campaign that goes door-to-door to mobilize voters might successfully contact every fourth person and generate votes at a rate of $19 per vote. This finding says something about the efficiency of that type of campaign, but it might not provide an accurate assessment of what would happen if your canvassers returned repeatedly to each house in an effort to contact three out of four voters. The cost of returning to each house might prove prohibitive, but the harvest of additional votes might offset these costs. It is hard to say. Be cautious when extrapolating to campaigns that are very different from the ones we have studied. Finally, special considerations sometimes come into play when assessing campaign costs. Depending on the specific campaign finance laws under which you are operating, you might have special financial incentives to spend dollars on one campaign tactic rather than another. Or you might know someone in the printing or telemarketing business willing to offer you a great deal. It is important to read the fine print of how we are calculating our cost-efficiency estimates so that you can tailor them to your particular situation.

campaigns face budget constraints. So the question is not What are some helpful campaign tactics? but rather What are the most cost-effective campaign tactics?

In order to know whether a campaign tactic is cost-effective, it is necessary to determine how many votes are produced for each dollar spent (see box 2-1). Most firms and organizations that offer campaign services or recommend campaign tactics have a fairly clear idea about the costs involved. Those experienced in running campaigns know the approximate unit cost of each mailer or phone call, the hourly rates of canvassers and supervisors, and the setup costs of producing literature and supervising these campaign operations. Indeed, one of the reasons that campaign professionals are valuable is that they possess an immense amount of knowledge about what it takes to execute a campaign. Seasoned campaign veterans know a great deal about the *inputs,* but they seldom possess reliable information about the *outputs:* the number of votes that these tactics produce.

Campaign professionals and candidates tell lots of war stories about the mailers that Candidate X distributed prior to winning a big upset victory or how Candidate Y squandered her big lead in the polls by failing to mobilize her base. These anecdotes do not enable you to isolate the influence of any particular input. They simply encourage you to imagine a counterfactual world in which the campaign behaved differently, while everything else about the campaign remained the same. The skeptic might well wonder: Was Candidate X's victory really due to mailers? Might something about Candidate Y have caused her campaign to run into trouble other than her alleged problems in mobilizing her core supporters?

In the nonpartisan world similarly unsubstantiated claims are voiced with respect to, for instance, voter registration. Massive voter registration drives are portrayed by their sponsors as grand successes. Press releases announce that thousands and sometimes hundreds of thousands of people were registered as part of this or that campaign. Even if you are prepared to believe the numbers, caution is warranted for two reasons. First, exciting as it may be to register large numbers of people, registration is not the same as voting. Second, the people who were registered as part of a big drive might have registered anyway on their own (or as part of a small, less publicized drive). As we show in chapter 7, nonpartisan campaigns sometimes register large numbers of people and yet fail to raise either the registration rate or the voting rate.

The problem of drawing sound conclusions from anecdotes persists even when campaign veterans are equipped with many, many war stories and perhaps even a statistical analysis to boot. It is sometimes quipped that the word "data" is plural for "anecdote." Suppose that voter turnout rates tend to be higher in districts where campaigns spend unusually large sums on professional phone banks. What would this say about the influence of phone banks on voter turnout? Not a whole lot. It could be that the same forces that bring a lot of money into campaigns—such as a tight race for an important office—are the very things that attract voter interest. We might observe a correlation between turnout and expenditures on professional phone banks even if calls from phone banks have no effect whatsoever on voter turnout.

Even fancy statistical analysis of survey data or historical voting patterns cannot overcome the basic principle that correlation is not causation. Suppose that you ask survey respondents to describe whether they were called by a campaign and whether they voted. The correlation between these two reports may be quite misleading. First, to put it politely, respondents may inaccurately recall whether they were contacted and whether they voted. Those who wish to present themselves as politically involved may be more likely to indicate both that they were contacted and that they voted. Second, campaigns often target likely voters. Even if canvassing had no effect, your survey would still reveal higher voting rates among the folks who were contacted. That is *why* they were contacted. Statistical fixes cannot resolve these problems without relying on untestable assumptions about response error and the targeting strategies used by campaigns. Complex statistical analysis creates a fog that is too often regarded as authoritative. When confronted with reams of impressive sounding numbers, it is easy to lose sight of the weak research design from which they emerged.

The situation is no better when scholars assemble historical data on voter turnout and attempt to tease out the effects of campaign tactics by "holding constant" various background factors. Suppose that voter turnout rates were unusually high in areas canvassed by labor unions. Does this pattern mean that canvassing increased turnout or that labor unions deployed their canvassers in areas with unusually high turnout?

The rigorous scientific study of voter mobilization requires something more than reams of data and impressive-sounding correlations. It requires a method for making fair comparisons between instances where a campaign tactic was or was not used. It requires a method for establishing that the people who were canvassed, phoned, or mailed were just like those who were left alone. Only one procedure ensures a fair comparison, and that is random assignment. Flip a coin to decide whether each person will be exposed to some form of "treatment" or instead assigned to a control group. Since every person has the same chance of getting into the treatment group, there will be no systematic tendency for the treatment group to contain a disproportionate number of frequent voters. As the number of people in the study increases, chance differences in the composition of the treatment and control groups will tend to disappear. When thousands of people are randomly assigned to treatment and control groups, experiments enable researchers to form a precise assessment of a treatment's impact.

What sets this book apart is that its conclusions about what campaign tactics work are based exclusively on evidence from randomized experiments. The remainder of this chapter provides some detail about how and where these experiments were conducted. If you are eager to hear about the conclusions of these studies, you may wish to skip this chapter and move on to chapter 3, but we encourage you to acquire at least some passing familiarity with experimental research. The more you understand about these studies, the easier it will be for you to recognize the strengths and limitations of the results when applying them to your own situation. Who knows? You may even be inspired to launch your own experiment.

Randomized Experiments

Randomized experimentation is a tool often used in medical research to gauge the effectiveness of new medications or treatment protocols. The reason is simple: in medical research, the stakes are enormous. Lives hang in the balance, and so do billions of dollars in pharmaceutical sales. In order to prevent profit-driven companies from exaggerating the claims of their products, the Food and Drug Administration maintains a very high standard of scientific rigor when evaluating new treatments.

Compared to the world of pharmaceuticals, the world of elections is free-wheeling and unregulated. No organization or agency monitors the quality of scientific claims. Randomized experiments are therefore about as rare in politics as successful third-party candidates.

Recognizing the importance of obtaining reliable evidence about how to increase voter turnout, we have made extensive use of randomized experimentation since 1998, and our work has inspired others to conduct experiments of their own. Dozens of experiments have been conducted at various points in the electoral calendar: presidential elections, federal midterm elections, state off-year elections, municipal elections, runoff elections, and party primaries. Some of these studies have taken place in states with traditional voting systems (such as New York), while others have occurred in early-voting states (Colorado) or in vote-by-mail-only states (Oregon). These get-out-the-vote campaigns have taken place in areas as different as Detroit, Columbus, and the rural outskirts of

Fresno. Many of these experiments have involved nonpartisan efforts to get people to the polls; some, however, have studied attempts by partisan campaigns to both mobilize and persuade voters.

Despite these differences, the randomized studies of voter turnout discussed in this volume have a common structure, which consists of six components.

✔ A population of observations is defined. This population includes all the people or geographically defined groups whose actions will be measured (whether they are exposed to the GOTV intervention or not). Most studies draw their sample from lists of registered voters, although a few studies draw samples from lists of streets or precincts.

✔ The observations are *randomly* divided into a treatment and a control group. Random assignment has a very specific meaning in this context. It does not refer to haphazard or arbitrary assignment. Special care is taken to ensure that every observation has the same chance of being assigned to the treatment group. In its most basic form, random assignment can be accomplished by flipping a coin for each individual, assigning all those who receive "heads" to the treatment group. In practice, random assignment is performed using a computerized random number generator.

✔ An intervention is applied to persons in the treatment group. For example, members of the treatment group may be sent mail encouraging them to vote.

✔ The outcome variable is measured for those in each group. In all of the studies we discuss, voting is measured by examining public records, *not* by asking people whether they voted. The percentage of people in the treatment group who voted is then compared to the percentage in the control group who voted.

✔ The difference in voting rates is subjected to statistical analysis. The aim is to determine how much uncertainty remains about the true effect of the intervention. The larger the study—that is, the greater the number of observations assigned to treatment and control groups—the less uncertainty will remain after the experiment is analyzed. Statistical analysis also takes into account one of the annoying facts about both campaigning and experimenting: sometimes it is not possible to reach the people being targeted. If researchers know the rate at which people were contacted, they can calculate how much influence the experimental intervention had on those who were contacted. Both facts are needed to gauge how effective this intervention is likely to be when used in the future.

✔ The experiment is replicated in other times and places. A single experiment can establish that a GOTV tactic works in a particular setting; a series of experiments is necessary to show that the experimental hypothesis holds when the political, economic, or demographic conditions are different. Replicating experiments also enables researchers to figure out whether variations in the way a treatment is administered affect the results.

Conducting studies of this kind requires campaign management skills—in two senses. First, many of the experiments were the product of campaigns that the researchers themselves developed or helped to coordinate. The original 1998 studies in New Haven and West Haven, Connecticut, involved door-to-door canvassing, direct mail, and professional phone banks. Our research team plotted out canvassing routes, oversaw dozens of precinct walkers, worked with direct mail vendors to create and distribute nine different mailers, devised phone scripts, and monitored the calls from the phone bank. (The fact that we, as novices, were able to pull this off with only a few glitches should hearten those of you about to embark on your first campaign.) Our study harkens back to a randomized field experiment conducted in the 1950s by Sam Eldersveld, a University of Michigan political scientist whose campaign skills later catapulted him to the position of mayor of Ann Arbor.

The second sense in which we use the term "campaign management" refers to the fact that many of the experiments we report grow out of collaborations with actual campaigns. We never turn down an opportunity to study campaigns experimentally and are proud to have worked with candidates and groups across the ideological spectrum: Republican campaigns for Congress, Democratic campaigns for state assembly and mayor, interest group campaigns designed to mobilize African Americans, and nonpartisan campaigns designed to mobilize Latinos and voters between the ages of eighteen and twenty-five. For these groups, mobilizing votes is understandably a higher priority than conducting research. Nevertheless, amid the time pressures of an impending election, these campaigns assigned a random portion of their target lists to a control group. Collaboration with actual campaigns has greatly enhanced our understanding of how various campaign tactics work under a range of real-world conditions.

Many things can go awry in the conduct of these experiments. If canvassers are allowed to choose which houses to visit, they may inadvertently administer the treatment to subjects in the control group. We take pains, therefore, to make sure that these experiments are carried out according to the randomized experimental protocols that we devised. We have conducted dozens of successful experiments but also several fiascos that had to be discarded because the experimental plan was not followed.

One final point bears emphasis. Although we have conducted a great many experiments and evaluations, we have not accepted money from the campaigns or interest groups whose efforts we have evaluated. When asked to maintain the anonymity of names and places, we have done so, but all of the experiments we conduct are arranged with the clear understanding that the results will be made public in a form that permits the accumulation of knowledge.

The Studies Described in This Book

This book reports the results of experiments conducted each year from 1998 through 2002. This section offers a brief chronology of the studies that we and others conducted during this period.

Federal Midterm Elections, 1998

Our first foray into the world of randomized field experiments was conducted in our own backyard. In an attempt to get away from students, however, we excluded the Yale ward from our study of New Haven. Under the auspices of the League of Women Voters, we created a non-partisan campaign called "Vote '98" and conducted three experiments. In New Haven, we designed and managed a door-to-door canvassing effort that spoke with more than 1,600 people. In New Haven and the neighboring city of West Haven, a commercial phone bank contacted more than 4,800 people. In New Haven, direct mail was sent to more than 11,000 households. Leftover copies of these 8.5" x 11" direct mail postcards were distributed as leaflets to randomly selected streets in the nearby town of Hamden during the final weekend before election day.

State and Municipal Elections, 1999

We returned to New Haven for a reprise of the direct mail campaign used a year earlier. Whereas in 1998 we randomly assigned households to receive no, one, two, or three mailings, in 1999 we raised the maximum number of mailings to eight in an effort to locate the point at which additional mailings would be fruitless. These mailings were again non-partisan, although we experimented with different content in order to determine whether the messages we used affected voter turnout. In a departure from nonpartisan mobilization drives, we collaborated with three Democratic candidates, one running for mayor of a small city and two running for state legislative seats in New Jersey. By randomly extracting a control group from their mailing lists, these campaigns were able to gauge the effects of partisan direct mail on voter turnout.

Presidential Elections, 2000

This year featured a wide array of experimental studies. Partisan direct mail was randomized in another state legislative campaign, this time on behalf of a Democratic candidate in Connecticut. A randomized evaluation was conducted of the NAACP National Voter Fund's multi-million-dollar direct mail and phone bank campaign, which, in conjunction with a media campaign and door-to-door efforts, was designed to mobilize African Americans in more than a dozen states. Although not explicitly partisan in character, the NAACP National Voter Fund's phone and direct mail campaign messages argued vehemently that then-governor George W. Bush was not the candidate who would best serve black interests. On the nonpartisan front, we performed randomized evaluations of Youth Vote 2000's efforts to mobilize young voters through phone calls and door-to-door canvassing. Finally, Youth Vote launched a pilot study designed to assess whether e-mail is successful in mobilizing young voters.

Municipal Elections, 2001

In the interest of corroborating our earlier findings about nonpartisan face-to-face canvassing across a variety of urban settings, we collaborated with a coalition of nonpartisan groups urging voter participation in municipal elections in Bridgeport, Columbus, Detroit, Minneapolis, Raleigh, and St. Paul. Moving this line of research outside of urban settings, Melissa Michelson of California State University, Fresno conducted a door-to-door mobilization campaign in the nearby, rural, and largely Latino community of Dos Palos. In Boston and Seattle, a series of phone bank experiments were conducted, one of which used pre-recorded calls from the local registrar of voters to remind residents to vote on election day.

Federal Midterm Elections, 2002

This election cycle saw a number of studies examining the effects of partisan campaign efforts. We conducted a randomized direct mail experiment in collaboration with a Republican congressional incumbent prior to the primary and general elections. Jennifer Steen of Boston College conducted a randomized study of the mail and phone bank efforts of a Republican state senator's reelection campaign. Our Yale collaborator John Lapinski conducted a randomized study of robo calls recorded by the Republican Party in King County, Washington.[5] Another Yale collaborator, David Nickerson, who oversaw the Youth Vote 2000 studies, teamed up with Ryan Friedrichs, a Harvard University student and party activist, to conduct a randomized evaluation of a campaign by the Michigan Democratic Party to mobilize young voters. John McNulty of University of California, Berkeley gauged the effects of a campaign's attempt to mobilize voters in opposition to a municipal ballot proposition in San Francisco.

Nonpartisan mobilization studies also grew increasingly refined in 2002. Melissa Michelson conducted another experiment in the Fresno area, this one designed to see whether Anglo and Latino canvassers were differentially effective in mobilizing Anglo and Latino voters. Janelle Wong of the University of Southern California examined whether various Asian ethnic groups in Los Angeles—Chinese, Indian, Japanese, Korean, Filipino—were stimulated to vote by direct mail and phone calls, many of which were conducted in languages other than English. Ricardo Ramírez, also of the University of Southern California, evaluated the phone canvassing and direct mail efforts of the National Association of Latino Elected Officials, a nonpartisan group that sought to mobilize Latino voters in four states using local phone banks, direct mail, and robo calls. Elizabeth Bennion of Indiana University, South Bend examined the effects of door-to-door canvassing in the context of a hotly contested congressional election. Finally, we conducted an evaluation of the nonpartisan organization Votes For Students, which attempted to mobilize more than 300,000 college students via e-mail.

GOTV Shoppers' Guide

As you make your way through this book, consider the applicability of these studies to your particular circumstances and goals. Think about whether the tactics that we reveal to be successful are feasible for you. For example, you may not have access to large numbers of canvassers or to the money needed to send out six pieces of direct mail. You may also want to think about whether you can tweak a strategy we discuss to fit your circumstances. If you cannot mount a door-to-door campaign, perhaps you can make face-to-face contact with voters in retirement homes, shopping centers, night schools, or religious centers. We have not studied these tactics directly, so there is more uncertainty about whether they work. Use your judgment when making the leap from our research findings to analogous situations that your campaign may encounter.

In order to help you to keep track of the uncertainty surrounding each of the lessons learned from the experimental studies, we have created a simple rating system.

★★★ A three-star rating indicates that the finding is based on experiments involving large numbers of voters and that the GOTV tactic has been implemented by different groups in a variety of sites.

★★ A two-star rating indicates that the finding is based on a small number of experiments. We have a reasonable level of confidence in the results but harbor some reservations because they have not been replicated across a wide array of political, demographic, or geographic conditions.

★ A one-star rating indicates that the finding is suggested by experimental evidence but not demonstrated conclusively in one or more studies.

For example, we have a rather clear impression of how well commercial phone banks mobilize voters when callers read a very brief script. Several truly massive experiments have estimated this effect with a great deal of precision. The results warrant three stars. Leafleting studies, in contrast, are much fewer in number, and just one nails down the effect of door hangers with precision. The leafleting result therefore warrants two stars. If we slice the data even more thinly, restricting attention to nonpartisan leafleting campaigns, the results become still more uncertain, warranting one star.

Keep in mind that we are only beginning to accumulate randomized trial data. As this book goes to press, we continue to plan and execute more studies. We continue to refine our current stock of knowledge and to broaden the range of campaign techniques that we have subjected to rigorous inquiry. Our research—like all research—is provisional and incomplete. Nevertheless, the findings reported here can help you to form realistic expectations about your GOTV campaign. How many votes would you realistically expect to generate as the result of 400,000 robo calls? How about 27,000 mailers? Or 2,800 conversations at voters' doorsteps? By the time you finish this book, you will understand why the answer is approximately 200.

CHAPTER THREE

Door-to-Door Canvassing:
Shoe Leather Politics

D oor-to-door canvassing was once the bread and butter of party mobilization, particularly in urban areas. Ward leaders made special
efforts to canvass their neighborhoods, occasionally calling in favors or
offering small financial incentives to ensure that their constituents delivered their votes on election day. Petty corruption was rife, but turnout
rates were high, even in relatively poor neighborhoods.

With the decline of patronage politics and the rise of technologies that
sharply reduced the cost of phone calls and mass mailings, shoe leather
politics gradually faded away. The shift away from door-to-door canvassing occurred not because this type of mobilization was discovered to
be ineffective, but rather because the economic and political incentives
facing parties, candidates, and campaign professionals changed over time.

Although local parties still tend to favor face-to-face mobilization,
state and national parties prefer campaign tactics that afford them centralized control over the deployment of campaign resources. The decentralized network of local ward heelers was replaced by phone banks and
direct mail firms, whose messages could be standardized and whose
operations could be started with very short lead time and deployed virtually anywhere on an enormous scale. National parties still conduct
"ground operations," but these activities account for a relatively small
share of their campaign outlays.

Candidates, too, gradually drifted away from door-to-door canvassing,
lured by the short lead times and minimal start-up costs of impersonal

campaigning. Furthermore, the ability to translate campaign funds directly into voter mobilization activities through private vendors selling direct mail and phone bank services meant that candidates were less beholden to local party activists. Candidates with money but without much affection for or experience with their party could run credible campaigns even in large jurisdictions.

Finally, a class of professional campaign consultants emerged to take advantage of the profits that could be made brokering direct mail, phone banks, and mass media. Less money was to be made from door-to-door canvassing, and campaign professionals had little incentive to invest in the on-the-ground infrastructure of local volunteers because there was no guarantee that these campaign professionals would be hired back to work in the same area.

You should therefore expect to get conflicting advice about the value of door-to-door canvassing. Campaign professionals, for example, sometimes belittle this type of campaign, because it is associated with candidates who are watching their budgets—in other words, candidates who are unattractive customers. Local party officials often swear by it, but because they are in a tug-of-war with the national parties for resources, local activists have an incentive to tout these activities.

We do not have a dog in this fight. In this chapter, we discuss the practical challenges of organizing a door-to-door campaign and review the results from a dozen experimental studies. The evidence leaves little doubt that door-to-door canvassing by campaign workers can increase turnout substantially, but the studies also show that mounting a canvassing campaign has its drawbacks. Successful campaigns require planning, motivated canvassers, and access to large numbers of residences. As you review the evidence, think about whether your campaign or organization has the ingredients for a successful and cost-efficient door-to-door campaign.

Organizing and Conducting a Door-to-Door Canvassing Campaign

Door-to-door canvassing encompasses a variety of activities that involve making direct contact with citizens. In partisan campaigns, for example, canvassing may be performed by candidates themselves, their campaign workers, or allied groups. The canvassers may distribute literature, absentee ballot applications, lawn signs, or other campaign paraphernalia.

On election day, canvassers may be equipped with cell phones to enable them to coordinate rides to the polls. Canvassing should be thought of not only as a means of getting out votes but also as a vehicle for recruiting campaign volunteers and improving the public visibility of a campaign.

Canvassing on a scale sufficient to reach thousands of voters over the span of three or four weeks requires extensive planning and organization. But even a small-scale canvassing effort requires a fair amount of preparation. When planning, it is often helpful to break the canvassing operation into a set of discrete tasks: targeting, recruiting, scheduling, training, and supervising.

Targeting

As with any get-out-the-vote effort, canvassing begins with a target population, that is, a set of potential voters whom you think it worthwhile to mobilize. For instance, your target voters might be all registered Republicans or Democrats who voted in the last general election or Latinos or Christian conservatives. It is important to think about what you need to do to find your target group. Can you just canvass certain neighborhoods, or do you need to identify the specific individuals or households that fit your target?

If the latter, you will need to begin by creating or purchasing an accurate list of potential voters (see boxes 3-1, 3-2, and 3-3 on obtaining, updating, and refining lists). Ideally, your list should be accurate in two ways. It should accurately reflect the pool of individuals you want to contact, and it should provide accurate contact information for those individuals. Maintaining an updated voter list is very important. You should enter the list into your computer and adjust it as information comes in. Suppose you are running as a Democrat. Some people listed as Democrats may no longer consider themselves Democrats. Some people, when canvassed, may indicate that they do not support you. In short, if you are planning to recontact people after your initial canvass, you should take the time to update your list.

The task of meeting people at their doorstep poses a variety of challenges. How accessible are the people on your target list? There is no sense wasting time cursing locked security apartments. When are the residents likely to be home? If most registered voters in the neighborhood work, your canvassers will have to wait until evenings or weekends to make efficient use of their time.

Box 3-1. How to Get Lists

In most jurisdictions, lists of registered voters are accessible to the public and generally are available from local registrars, county clerks, and secretaries of state. The costs of these lists vary wildly across jurisdictions. You may pay $5 or $500. Depending on your needs and resources, you may also want to hire a private list vendor or work with a political party or organization that maintains lists. Lists of registered voters always contain names and addresses and sometimes contain other information that could be useful to a canvassing effort such as voter history (whether an individual has voted in the last one, two, or more elections), party registration, sex, and birth date. In some jurisdictions, these records also include phone number, although this information is often out of date. In states covered by the Voting Rights Act, registration lists indicate the race of each voter.

If you plan to canvass in the evenings, consider the safety of your canvassers. By late October it may be getting dark before 7:00 p.m., and residents may react poorly to an evening visit from a stranger. You do not want to frighten or offend the potential voter you are trying to engage. You should instruct your canvassers to take a step back away from the door after ringing the bell so that they will seem less threatening to apprehensive residents. It is sometimes argued that people are more willing to open their door to female canvassers; it turns out, however, that the gender composition of a canvassing team is a poor predictor of the rate at which voters are contacted. Well-trained teams with two males, a

---

Box 3-2. Adding Extra Information to Lists

For a fee, list vendors usually can provide two additional pieces of information that can be useful to door-to-door campaigns: four-digit zip code extensions (which identify addresses in small clusters) and mail carrier route numbers (which can be used to create geographically compact walk lists). When requesting or purchasing any list, it is important to find out when the lists were last updated. Whenever possible, get the list in electronic form so that you can manipulate and update the data easily.

Box 3-3. Refining the List

There are three ways to pare down a list to include only the subgroup you would like to canvass. Information on a particular ethnic or socioeconomic sector of the voting population is available from the U.S. Census at its website: www.census.gov. Although you cannot get information about individual households, you can get information about census blocks, the smallest geographic area delineated by the census. This will allow you to determine, for instance, which neighborhoods in a particular district have a high concentration of, say, homeowners or Asians or people living below the poverty line. You can then pull the names of registrants from those neighborhoods for your canvassing effort or just canvass those neighborhoods in their entirety, if you have reason to believe that doing so would be efficient.

List vendors can also help with ethnic targeting, for a price. Private firms have name-matching software that allows them to pull names that tend to be associated with a particular ethnicity or nationality. A firm may be able to provide a list of registered voters in a given district whose last names are typically Latino or Chinese, for example. If all else fails, you can team up with ethnic or religious groups that maintain mailing lists that might serve as targets for your campaign. Since those lists do not indicate whether the individuals are registered, you will need to match them against the registration files.

Although the voter file does not say how a person voted, it often contains information about each person's party registration and record of voting in previous elections. Voting in closed primaries usually provides good clues about a person's partisan leanings. These clues can be useful when developing a targeted GOTV campaign.

male and female, or two females tend, on average, to have about the same success in reaching voters.

Because there are so many contingencies, and so many details that can throw a wrench into your plans, it might make sense to prioritize your walk lists. This entails choosing the most essential neighborhoods and making sure that they get covered. You may want to get to them first, in order to ensure that they have been reached, or you may want to visit them right before the election, in order to ensure that your message is fresh in voters' minds on election day.

Recruiting Activists and Paid Volunteers

Unlike professional phone banks and direct mail, canvassing is almost entirely dependent on labor that, one way or another, you will have to produce. High schools and colleges are good sources of labor, particularly when students know the neighborhoods in which they will be working. Other sources of labor include churches, civic groups, unions, and interest groups such as the Sierra Club or National Rifle Association.

There are, of course, advantages and disadvantages to forging an alliance with a social or political group that supports your candidate or shares a common political goal with your campaign. Any organization that becomes an ally has its own agenda. By collaborating on a GOTV partnership, you may be tacitly endorsing your ally's politics, and the canvassers it supplies may have difficulty staying on message for you. In addition, if the partnership is seen as a personal favor, then a favor may be expected in return. The decision to collaborate may hinge on whether your ally will supply enough canvassing labor to make an alliance worthwhile.

Scheduling

Across a range of studies, we have found that canvassers typically contact five to eight registered voters per hour. Although the number of doors knocked on per hour will vary depending on residential density, the number of successful contacts per hour has proven to be quite consistent. This pattern suggests that people living in low-density detached housing are more likely to be at home than people living in apartment complexes. Canvassers can even wade through neighborhoods a second time, attempting to contact voters missed on an earlier attempt, without much loss in efficiency.

This rate of contact per hour is a very conservative estimate of what you are likely to experience when canvassing. When we conduct experiments, we assign half of the potential targets to the control group and remove them from the walk lists. Canvassers have to walk farther in order to reach the home of the next person on their list. Unless you are conducting an experiment, your canvassers will not be subject to this constraint. A more realistic rate of contact for an actual campaign is twelve contacts per hour.[1]

This twelve-per-hour rate allows you to calculate how many hours of labor you will need for the campaign. Simply divide the number of con-

---

Box 3-4. Calculating the Number of Canvassing Hours Needed per Week

Ms. Smith is running for mayor and sets out to contact 3,600 voters in targeted areas. Dividing 3,600 contacts by twelve contacts per hour means that she needs 300 work hours. If her canvassing campaign is spread evenly over the three-week period leading up to the election, each week must total 100 canvassing hours. Depending on the size and reliability of her labor pool, she can fill 100 hours using many canvassers working briefly or a few working continually.

---

tacts desired by the average of twelve contacts per hour. The resulting quotient is the number of volunteer hours required. Then divide the number of total canvassing hours into the number of weeks over which the canvassing will take place to obtain an average number of canvassing hours per week. Volunteers typically can be counted on to work two-hour shifts. The number of available shifts in a week varies from region to region, but most campaigns conduct their canvassing efforts from 5:00 to 7:00 p.m. on weeknights and from 10:00 a.m. to 5:00 p.m. on Saturdays. Sunday afternoon canvassing depends entirely on the region and population but seldom takes place outside the hours of 1:00 to 5:00 p.m. This accounting—a total of ten hours on the five weeknights, seven hours on Saturday, and four hours on Sunday—allows for up to ten shifts per week. Given the number of shifts per week and the number of hours per shift, you can now calculate the number of canvassing hours needed per week (see box 3-4).

Safety

Unlike more impersonal GOTV tactics, door-to-door canvassing can place volunteers at some personal risk. However, you can minimize risk and increase the effectiveness of the campaign in six ways. First, you can send canvassers out in pairs. Each canvasser should go to separate doors, but they can do this while remaining near enough to each other (by working opposite sides of the street or visiting alternating addresses) that they will be able to see or hear if the other encounters a problem. Sending workers out in pairs has the added benefit of providing some assurance that the canvassers are actually doing what they are supposed to, especially if you pair trusted canvassers with unknown quantities.

Second, you should provide canvassers with maps of their assigned areas so they do not get lost. Third, you should provide canvassers with an emergency number so that they can call you in the event they encounter a problem. Ideally, at least one canvasser in the group should be equipped with a cell phone. Fourth, whenever possible, you should assign canvassers to neighborhoods with which they are familiar. Not only will canvassers be less likely to face a problem in a familiar neighborhood, but familiarity also should strengthen their personal connection to the voters—something that may prove beneficial in getting those who are contacted to vote. Fifth, you should give canvassers something to identify them as canvassers and not marauders (whom they may sometimes resemble). For example, it is helpful for canvassers to wear a campaign T-shirt or campaign button. They also can put a campaign bumper sticker on the back of their clipboard, so that residents see it when they peek out of their door. Finally, you should require all canvassers to reconvene at a predetermined time and location so that you can count heads. Reconvening all canvassers at the conclusion of the shift also allows you to collect the walk lists and verify their work.

Weather sometimes presents safety and efficiency concerns of its own. Getting stuck in a downpour or an unexpected snow squall can leave canvassers demoralized, not to mention cold and wet. It is useful to discuss ahead of time the contingency plans that will go into effect in case of bad weather. In principle, poor weather presents a good opportunity for canvassing, since more people can be found at home, but the success of the operation hinges on whether canvassers have umbrellas and plastic sheets to protect their walk lists.

Training

Door-to-door canvassing is a simple technique that anyone willing to knock on a stranger's door can be taught to do. Interestingly enough, experiments have shown that experienced canvassers tend to be only slightly more effective than newcomers. The power of canvassing stems from the personal connection that face-to-face communication provides. Training of volunteer canvassers does not need to be extensive. A half-hour session should include the following:

✔ An explanation of the purpose of the canvass,
✔ Precise instruction on what to say and do at each door,

Box 3-5. Script of a Message
Directed toward Latino Voters

A door-to-door campaign in Fresno, California, included some messages directed specifically toward Latino voters:

> Hi. My name is [your name], and I'm a student at Fresno State. I want to talk to you a few minutes about the upcoming elections on Tuesday, November 5. [Canvassers were then asked to talk briefly about the following points]:
>
> ✔ Voting gives the Latino community a voice.
>
> ✔ Your vote helps your family and neighbors by increasing Latino political power.
>
> ✔ Voting tells politicians to pay attention to the Latino community.

Canvassers closed their conversation by asking voters whether they could be counted on to vote on Tuesday.

✔ Division of volunteers into pairs and the assignment of a canvassing area to each pair,

✔ An opportunity for each canvasser to practice the script with his or her partner, preferably under the supervision of someone who will coach canvassers not to recite the script in a canned fashion,

✔ Distribution of all necessary materials, such as clipboards, walk lists, maps, and pens,

✔ Explanation of what information each canvasser should record after an address is visited,

✔ At least one phone number to call in the event of an emergency, and

✔ Designation of a time and location at which all canvassers will meet up at the end of the shift.

The message given in door-to-door canvassing should be consistent with the message of the overall campaign. The written pitch provided to volunteers should be treated more as a rough guideline than as a script to be read verbatim (see box 3-5). As we show in the chapter on phone banks, an informal style of communicating with potential voters works best. Scripts are necessary to provide guidance and confidence for inexperienced personnel, but the goal is not to create an army of automatons mindlessly parroting the same words. Encourage canvassers to make their presentations in words that are compatible with their own informal speaking style. This will help them to convey their message in a manner that increases the listener's motivation to vote.

When done properly, canvassing opens a conversation with voters. Prepare your canvassers to field some questions that voters might throw at them. The more comfortable canvassers feel conversing with voters, the better.

Supervising

Once the canvassers take to the streets, problems may range from bashfulness to drunkenness. Campaign managers have developed a number of tactics for monitoring the progress of canvassers, particularly those who are working for hourly wages. First, have them fill out the names of the people they meet at each door they visit. Since this report conceivably could be faked (although claims to have contacted an unusually large number of people would raise a red flag), another useful tactic is to send canvassers out with lawn signs or placards advertising the campaign. The goal is to convince residents to plant the signs in their yard or to put posters in their window; seeing who can plant the most signs can be a useful source of friendly competition among canvassers. This visible indicator of success makes it easy for a supervisor to see where canvassers have been and to gauge how they are doing.

Nowadays, cell phones are sufficiently cheap and plentiful to enable every canvasser to have one. Although it is unwise for their phones to be turned on—lest canvassers spend their day gabbing with friends—you should instruct them to call in at scheduled times and in case of trouble or questions. If canvassers depend on you for rides to the canvassing area, cell phones can help you to coordinate pickup times and locations.

Payment for services is best done on a weekly rather than an on-the-spot basis. First, weekly payment schedules encourage canvassers to think of this activity as an ongoing commitment. Second, it gives you a chance to discuss their performance with them after a day on the job, while they are still thinking about the payment that they expect to receive in the future.

Finally, you must take responsibility for dealing with unexpected events. The most common problem, at least in some parts of the country, is bad weather. Along with clipboards containing maps and address lists, canvassers should carry plastic covers in case of rain. A backup supply of umbrellas will keep the canvassing campaign from dissolving in a downpour. Besides weather problems, you should expect to field an occasional follow-up call from a resident, building manager, or local politician wondering what your campaign is up to. Think of canvassing as a big walk through town, a meet-and-greet with thousands of strangers. The outcomes are generally positive, but anything can happen.

Experimental Research on Door-to-Door Canvassing

More than a dozen door-to-door canvassing experiments have been conducted since 1998. Although the nature and scope of these campaigns varied from place to place, they shared many common elements. Registered voters in targeted neighborhoods were placed randomly into treatment and control groups. Canvassers were put through roughly a half hour of training, given a list of target names and addresses, and instructed to speak only to voters on their target list.[2] The particular GOTV pitches used by the canvassers varied from experiment to experiment (we discuss these variations momentarily), but the communication was designed to be informal and personal. In some cases, canvassers also distributed campaign material, voter guides, or information about polling locations.

The canvassing experiments can be grouped into three broad categories. The first encompasses nonpartisan canvassing efforts that were orchestrated by college professors. Such studies occurred in Dos Palos (a farm community in central California), Fresno, New Haven, and South Bend.[3] The second category includes door-to-door campaigns that were organized and conducted by nonpartisan groups such as Youth Vote and issue advocacy groups such as ACORN (Association of Community Organizations for Reform Now) and PIRG (Public Interest Research Group).[4] Academics helped to randomize the walk lists used by these canvassers but otherwise played a minor role. This type of canvassing occurred in Boulder, Bridgeport, Columbus, Detroit, Eugene, Minneapolis, Raleigh, and St. Paul. The final category includes precinct walking conducted by partisan organizations. Here we have just one campaign, a GOTV effort funded by the Michigan Democratic Party, which targeted young voters in approximately a dozen assembly districts.[5] In every site, the canvassers were ordinary people, not candidates running for office.

As this list of sites makes apparent, these experiments were conducted in a wide array of political and demographic settings. The precincts canvassed in Detroit were largely African American, whereas canvassers in

Columbus and Eugene rarely encountered nonwhites. Bridgeport and Fresno contained large Latino populations, and the areas canvassed in Minneapolis and St. Paul were surprisingly multiethnic. The suburban areas of Raleigh and the rural precincts of Dos Palos stood in marked contrast to the urban environments of Detroit or St. Paul. The political climate also varied across sites. Bridgeport, Columbus, and Dos Palos were canvassed amid uncompetitive municipal elections. Somewhat more competitive were elections in Minneapolis and New Haven, where at least some of the races featured credible challengers. By contrast, South Bend was canvassed amid a hotly contested congressional campaign, which saw both parties engaging in door-to-door campaigning. Detroit, Raleigh, and St. Paul were also canvassed during the last two weeks of closely contested mayoral elections.

Lessons Learned

The lessons emerging from these studies are rated according to the system detailed in chapter 2: three stars are for findings that have received solid confirmation from several experiments, two stars are for more equivocal findings based on one or two experiments, and one star is for findings that are suggestive but not conclusive.

★★★ *Canvassing generates votes.* These experiments suggest that, as a rule of thumb, one additional vote is produced for every fourteen people who are successfully contacted by canvassers. Here "contact" is defined rather broadly to include not only direct conversations with targeted voters but also conversations with their housemates requesting that they remind everyone in the household to vote. And this figure assumes that the base rate of voter turnout is somewhere between 25 and 75 percent. When turnout is extremely high or low, this rule of thumb must be adjusted a bit—see figure A-1 in appendix A.

To give you some sense of how the one-for-fourteen rule plays out across the various sites, the following number of contacts was needed to produce one additional vote in various places and types of elections: Bridgeport municipal, seven; Columbus municipal, ten; Denver municipal primary, twelve; Detroit mayoral, thirteen; Dos Palos municipal, twenty-three; Fresno federal midterm, twenty-eight; Michigan federal midterm, six; Minneapolis mayoral, ten; New Haven federal midterm, eleven; St. Paul mayoral, seven. The laggard of the bunch, the Fresno study, produced a statistically significant increase in turnout of 3.6 percentage points, which does not sound like much, except that only 8 percent of the control group voted.[6] Two studies—one in Raleigh (mayoral special election) and the other in South Bend (federal midterm election)—found that canvassing had no effect for reasons that we discuss below. Putting all the experiments together and taking into account the fact that some experiments were much larger in scope than others produces an average of one-for-fourteen. Another way to think about it is that canvassing "worked" in ten of the twelve sites where it was attempted, producing statistically significant gains in voter turnout.

★★★ *Canvassing is effective both in competitive and uncompetitive electoral settings.* We find big canvassing effects in the landslide elections in Bridgeport, where little was at stake and many candidates ran unopposed. We also see substantial effects in the closely contested mayoral elections that were held in Detroit and St. Paul. It appears that canvassers can successfully motivate citizens to participate in the electoral process across a range of electoral conditions.

★ *A GOTV canvassing effort may be less effective if conducted in areas that are being canvassed by other campaigns.* One caveat to the principle that canvassing can increase voter turnout in competitive races is that some races are so hot that your canvassing campaign duplicates the efforts of others. This explanation may account for the failure of the nonpartisan canvassing campaign in South Bend prior to the 2002 elections. Battling over a contested congressional seat, both parties apparently canvassed the same turf chosen by the nonpartisan campaign, which may have caused voters to become saturated with GOTV appeals. Interestingly, the one group responding positively to this nonpartisan campaign was voters eighteen to twenty-five years of age, a group that typically is ignored by partisan campaigns.

★★★ *Contacting eligible voters can be difficult.* If your campaign is trying to reach a target group that frequently changes address—young voters living off-campus, for example—expect to reach roughly one in five of the people you are looking for on each pass through the neighborhood. On the other hand, many groups (elderly voters, for example) have stable home addresses and are easy to find at home. The Dos Palos study gives a sense of the maximum rate of contact that a GOTV campaign can expect to achieve. After combing the town for two weeks, making multiple attempts to contact each name on the target list, this campaign met up with three out of four voters it sought to target.

★ *The messenger matters.* Canvassers who "match" the ethnic profile of the neighborhood tend to have more success than those who do not. One canvassing campaign noteworthy for its ineffectiveness at mobilizing voters occurred in Raleigh, North Carolina, where black and white canvassers attempted to canvass a predominantly white suburban neighborhood. According to canvassers' reports, some white residents refused to open their door to black canvassers. Two black canvassers were accosted by white residents and told to leave the neighborhood. A coincidental and concurrent canvassing effort by white supremacists seeking to deport Arabs raised residents' general level of hostility to canvassers, and local police stopped and questioned some of the white canvassers, thinking them to be part of the white supremacist effort.

Other studies provide mixed support for the notion that canvassers who match their targets have better success. In Dos Palos, a team of Latino Democrat canvassers were randomly assigned to canvass Anglo or Latino registered voters. The effects of canvassing were greater when these canvassers talked to Latino Democrats than to Latino non-Democrats or to non-Latinos. In contrast, the Fresno experiment in 2002, which involved both Latino and non-Latino canvassers and a target population of voters eighteen to twenty-five years of age, showed no consistent pattern. It may be that canvassing by those perceived to be "outsiders" is less threatening to young voters than to older and perhaps more ethnically conservative members of the electorate.

★★ *The message does not seem to matter much.* Experimenters have tried many variations on the door-to-door canvassing theme. Canvassers have distributed voter guides or polling place information. Canvassing scripts have emphasized neighborhood solidarity, ethnic solidarity, civic duty, and the closeness of the election. Although we cannot rule out the possibility that these variations in message and presentation make some difference, the effects seem to be so small that none of the studies was able to detect them reliably. We do not doubt—even without the benefit of experimental data!—that running door-to-door in a chicken suit or mentioning your support for outlandish political causes would undermine your effectiveness, but within the range of reasonable behaviors, we do not see much evidence that what you communicate matters.

Although we have concluded that the message does not matter very much, the data do suggest that some tactics might bump up turnout by a percentage point or two. One tactic is to ask citizens whether they can be counted on to vote. Another is to provide citizens with the location of their polling place. These effects are small, and we cannot claim to have isolated them with great precision, but they seem worth incorporating into most canvassing campaigns. Asking people whether they can be counted on to vote is virtually costless. Locating polling places requires a bit of effort, but not a whole lot. In general, we find that canvassers feel more comfortable conversing with people if they have information to convey and campaign paraphernalia to distribute, so nuances like providing polling information and asking for a commitment to vote may increase the effectiveness of canvassing simply by changing the tenor and length of the conversation on the doorstep.

★★★ *In low-turnout elections, such as municipal elections, canvassing tends to have greater effects on regular voters than on infrequent voters.* This fact may seem counterintuitive. You might suppose that frequent voters would be harder to influence simply because they are likely to vote anyway. But when we look more closely at these experimental results, we find that in Bridgeport, Columbus, Denver, Dos Palos, Fresno, Michigan, Minneapolis, and St. Paul, canvassing worked best among individuals who had voted in the preceding general election. In New Haven and Raleigh, canvassing worked equally well among frequent and infrequent voters. In Detroit and South Bend, infrequent voters responded more strongly to the canvassing drive than frequent voters. So the scorecard looks like this: frequent voters responded more strongly than intermittent voters in eight studies and less strongly in two studies, with two ties. Combining all of the studies of municipal and midterm elections, we find that canvassing is more than twice as effective at mobilizing people who voted in the last federal election than people who failed to do so, a difference that is too stark to be attributed to chance.

Not only are frequent voters typically more responsive to personal canvassing, they are also easier to contact. In every one of the studies, frequent voters were contacted at higher rates than infrequent voters. Thus, if the costs of approaching the two groups were the same, focusing on frequent voters would typically be more cost-effective. A few words of caution are in order, however. If you are walking a precinct, it may not pay to bypass a door simply because infrequent voters live there. You have already paid the setup cost of the canvassing operation; the extra costs of contacting infrequent voters might still pay off, particularly if you think your campaign is especially effective in reaching out to the infrequent voter. Remember, too, that cost-efficiency is not everything. If your group or campaign takes as its mission the mobilization of infrequent voters, your task is challenging, but certainly not impossible.

★★ *Door-to-door canvassing allows a campaign to influence people incidentally and indirectly.* One attractive feature of knocking on doors is that it provides an opportunity to converse with multiple voters living at the same address. The canvasser first talks to the person who answers the door and then asks to speak to the targeted voter. Everyone is told the purpose of the visit: the importance of the upcoming election.

In part, the rise in voting among nontargeted people reflects the fact that canvassers give their GOTV message to everyone who comes to the door, but that is not the only thing that is going on. Using a clever experiment, David Nickerson demonstrated that voters living at the same address also mobilize each other.[7] Nickerson led a canvassing effort that knocked on doors and gave a message only to the person who answered the door. Half of the messages were get-out-the-vote appeals; the other half, reminders to recycle. No messages were delivered to others in the household, yet other registered voters in households receiving the GOTV appeal voted at higher rates! Evidently, those who received the GOTV message communicated something about the upcoming election to others in their household. In light of this experiment and other evidence suggesting that canvassing affects both the intended targets and other voters in the household, the usual one-for-fourteen rule probably understates the effectiveness of door-to-door canvassing.

All in all, we see strong evidence that canvassing generates votes. Canvassing seems particularly effective when aimed at frequent voters who otherwise might skip a low-turnout election. Extra bells and whistles, such as providing polling place information or inviting people to make a verbal commitment to vote, may enhance slightly the effectiveness of door-to-door campaigns, although this conclusion remains tentative. Finally, canvassing campaigns seem to encourage people to talk about the upcoming election with others in the household, which has the effect of extending the influence of a canvassing campaign beyond those who are contacted directly.

Cost-Effectiveness

When you are evaluating the costs and benefits of canvassing, here are a few things to keep in mind. First, canvassing involves start-up costs. It takes time to plot out walking routes. If you intend to target specific individuals (as opposed to conducting a blanket GOTV campaign of all the residents living on certain streets), you need to obtain a registration list. You may want to hire a supervisor to recruit and coordinate canvassers. You may wish to send out your team of canvassers wearing the campaign's T-shirts and armed with maps, clipboards, printed material, buttons, or refrigerator magnets, all of which require some up-front investment. High-tech walking campaigns nowadays use small handheld computers to record and transmit data about every canvassing target.

Second, what counts as a "benefit" depends on your goals! The accounting we perform in this section considers only one goal: getting out votes. Using canvassers to persuade voters to vote in a certain way may generate extra benefits as well. Indeed, canvassing potentially provides all sorts of collateral benefits: canvassers receive useful feedback from voters about issues and candidates; the lawn signs and campaign buttons that canvassers distribute may help to publicize the campaign and communicate its message; canvassers can help to clean up an outdated target list of voters, weeding out the names of people who have moved; as canvassers go door-to-door, they can register new voters; and, by conversing with people about the campaign, canvassers can help to create databases of residents who are sympathetic to a given candidate and therefore warrant special GOTV efforts on election day. We have not attempted to quantify these extra returns to canvassing. So consider the cost-benefit analysis that follows as a conservative assessment of the strengths of canvassing.

The number of votes produced per dollar is a function of labor costs, the number of people contacted per hour, and the effectiveness with which a canvasser mobilizes the people contacted. According to Susan Burnside, a consultant who specializes in canvassing campaigns, the usual wage rate for canvassers varies from $6 to $16. In order to err on the side of caution, let's assume $16. If you are paying canvassers $16 per hour to contact twelve people per hour, you are, in effect, paying $1.33 per contact. Applying the one-for-fourteen rule, you need $18.67 worth of labor to produce one additional vote. You may cut labor costs dramatically by convincing a team of canvassers to work all afternoon in exchange for a dinner of pizza and beer (depending on how much they eat and drink). Similarly, an unusually energetic and persuasive group of canvassers may increase the number of voters per dollar, just as a hard-to-canvass neighborhood may decrease it. On the other hand, training, supervision, and infrastructure drive costs up, so your campaign might encounter substantially higher costs per vote.

If you are canvassing by yourself or are using unpaid volunteers, you may find it helpful to look at the efficiency problem in terms of the number of hours required to produce one vote. Twelve contacts per hour and fourteen contacts per vote produce one additional vote every seventy minutes. Generating a serious number of votes requires a serious investment of canvassing hours.

Assessment and Conclusions

Door-to-door canvassing is the tactic of choice among candidates and campaigns that are short on cash. Precinct walking is often described as the secret weapon of underdogs. One often hears stories of overmatched challengers who have used door-to-door canvassing to upset incumbents who have grown out of touch with their constituents. This chapter lends scientific support to the idea that face-to-face contact with voters raises turnout. Although we have yet to study the effects of candidates themselves going door-to-door, there is every reason to believe that candidates are as effective as volunteers, if not more so. We encourage readers to think of the cost-efficiency of face-to-face canvassing as a benchmark against which to compare other campaign tactics.

That said, canvassing door-to-door has its limitations. Precinct walking can be difficult and even dangerous. Anyone who has butted heads with managers of security apartments knows that some neighborhoods are inaccessible to political campaigns, notwithstanding court decisions that distinguish canvassing from commercial solicitation. Rural areas are often more hospitable, but the distance between houses undercuts the campaign's cost-efficiency. Perhaps the biggest challenge is bringing a door-to-door campaign "to scale." It is one thing to canvass 3,600 voters; quite another to canvass 36,000 or 360,000. It is rare for a campaign to inspire (or hire) a work force sufficient to canvass a significant portion of a U.S. House district, although the massive ground efforts by the Republican Party in the 2002 congressional elections remind us that large-scale precinct work is possible. A million dollars is not a particularly large sum by the standards of federal elections; media campaigns gobble up this amount in the production and distribution of a single ad. But a million dollars will hire an army of canvassers. Even if your campaign wins only your canvassers' families' affections and no one else's, the number of votes produced would be considerable.

The demonstrated effects of door-to-door canvassing suggest that other face-to-face tactics may stimulate voter turnout: shaking hands at a local supermarket, meeting voters at house parties, conversing with congregants at a church bingo night. We do not have direct evidence about the effectiveness of these time-honored campaign tactics, but they share much in common with conversations on a voter's doorstep. Face-to-face interaction makes politics come to life and helps voters to establish a personal connection with the electoral process. The canvasser's willingness to devote time and energy signals the importance of participation in the electoral process. Many nonvoters need just a nudge to motivate them to vote. A personal invitation sometimes makes all the difference.

CHAPTER FOUR

Leaflets:
Walk, Don't Talk

Leafleting is a get-out-the-vote tactic that shares much in common with door-to-door canvassing. Teams of canvassers comb neighborhoods, dropping literature at the doorstep (or inside the screen door) of targeted households. Like door-to-door canvassing, leafleting requires you to recruit and manage a pool of canvassers and to deal with the vagaries of bad weather, confusing street maps, and the like. But leafleting is easier, faster, and considerably less demanding than door-to-door canvassing. Just about anyone can do it, even those too shy to knock on doors. Leaflets can be distributed at just about any time of day, which vastly increases the number of hours that can be devoted to this activity during the final stages of a campaign.

Unfortunately, finding a leaflet at one's door tends to be a less memorable experience than having a face-to-face conversation with a canvasser. So the question of whether to distribute leaflets comes down to a matter of cost-efficiency. Does the extra coverage of a leafleting campaign offset the drop in effectiveness? This chapter strives to answer that question.

Organizing a Leaflet Campaign

Although leafleting campaigns require less preparation than door-to-door canvassing efforts, planning is still an essential ingredient for success. Designing an effective leaflet, organizing walk lists, and assembling a corps of leafleteers require time and energy. If you wait until the last moment, the quality and distribution of your literature will suffer. Here are some things to consider as you craft your leafleting campaign.

Leaflet Design

A leaflet campaign starts with the leaflet itself. Unless you have something worthwhile to distribute, there is little point in recruiting, deploying, and supervising a team of leafleteers. Many of the same principles that we discuss in the context of direct mail apply to leaflets:

✔ Use a visually engaging layout to encourage recipients to glance at the leaflet before throwing it away.

✔ Convey a simple, clear message in large print so that the gist of your message is apparent at a glance.

✔ Give the message credibility by including more detailed information for interested readers, perhaps directing them to a phone number or website.

Although nothing prevents you from producing leaflets using a desktop publisher, bear in mind that leaflets found lying on the ground in front of the doormat are less likely to attract attention than so-called door hangers. Door hangers, as the name suggests, have a perforated hole in the top that allows them to be hung on a doorknob.

The lead time required to produce a leaflet depends on its sophistication. The easiest approach is to produce a generic leaflet for distribution to everyone. At the other end of the spectrum are leaflets customized for the recipients, perhaps listing their polling place or making a voting appeal tailored to their demographic profile. Somewhere in the middle are leaflets tailored to voting precincts; these might provide polling place information but not a message aimed at an individual recipient. This last approach is easy for even a low-tech campaign to pull off; just use adhesive labels or rubber stamps to put polling place information on each leaflet.

Voter Lists

Not all leafleting campaigns require target lists. Some campaigns are content to drop their literature at every household, regardless of whether it contains registered voters. Sometimes these "blind canvassing" efforts are used because they serve other purposes, such as encouraging voter registration or publicizing an event or organization. Sometimes they are used by necessity, because canvassers are too young or unreliable to follow a walk list. Blind canvassing speeds up the process of visiting addresses because canvassers need only check which street they are on. For suburban neighborhoods with high registration rates, blind canvassing is often an efficient way to go. In areas with low registration rates, such as urban apartment complexes, blind canvassing may waste quite a bit of time and paper.

More sophisticated leafleting campaigns require database management. Printing customized leaflets, for example, requires a current voter registration list (see chapter 3 on how to obtain and prepare such lists). Even if you plan to use a generic leaflet for everyone in your target population, you need to obtain a registration list and sort it by street or carrier route. Assign each canvasser a set of contiguous carrier routes. As leafleteers return from each day's work, you should update these computer records to indicate where canvassers have visited.

The decision whether to canvass by street or by address in part depends on the purpose of the leafleting campaign. Some partisan leaflets are designed to mobilize voters, in which case it makes little sense to leave them at the doorstep of people registered in the opposing party. Other leaflets are intended to build a candidate's name recognition and communicate positive information about him or her. Unless you fear that these messages will produce a backlash among voters registered in the opposing party, you may distribute these leaflets blindly. If you are unsure about the likely effect of your partisan leaflets, it is probably safer to focus on people who either are registered in your party or are undeclared. That means targeting specific addresses.

Canvassers

Distributing leaflets is a low-skill activity and one that is often assigned to teenagers. You do not need to train canvassers to deliver a script, but you should provide instructions about what to say if they encounter someone as they proceed from address to address. A bit of guidance should be given about where and how to position the leaflet on someone's property. It is a bad idea to place leaflets in mailboxes, since legally they are the special domain of the postal service. In general, leaflets should be placed in ways that prevent them from blowing around and becoming litter. (They teeter on the edge of litter even under optimal conditions.)

Many of the same safety principles discussed in the previous chapter apply here. One further issue warrants mention. Leafleteers occasionally have the opportunity to sabotage other leafleting campaigns. On the day before the election, a leafleteer might encounter a large stack of competing leaflets on a resident's doorstep. To prevent unpleasant confrontations with other campaigns, you might discourage your canvassers from discarding or destroying these competing messages, urging them instead to place your message at the top of the stack.

Assessing the Effectiveness of Leaflets

Two experimental studies—one partisan and one nonpartisan—have looked at the extent to which leaflets stimulate voter turnout. The partisan study was crafted by Ryan Friedrichs and David King of Harvard and David Nickerson of Yale.[1] In this campaign, the Michigan Democratic Party targeted young voters in thirteen Michigan assembly districts during the weeks leading up to the 2002 general elections. This study involved a very large number of registered voters, roughly 2,500 in each assembly district. Because Michigan's registration system no longer includes a declaration of party, the canvassing campaign targeted voters eighteen to thirty-five, although the campaign focused on predominantly Democratic neighborhoods and excluded voters who had registered Republican under the previous registration system. The Michigan experiment used a door hanger that conveyed a partisan message, encouraged voter turnout, and listed the polling place for residents of a given ward (see figure 4-1). Thus the leaflet was customized for each precinct, but not each individual. Canvassers were instructed to deposit their door hangers only at certain addresses.

During the final days of the 1998 campaign, we conducted a nonpartisan experiment in the suburban town of Hamden, Connecticut.[2] Streets in the town were randomly assigned to treatment and control groups, and leafleteers distributed 8.5" x 11" postcards to every house on a treatment group street. Since this procedure was tantamount to a blind canvass, efficiency was compromised a bit, but in these neighborhoods a very high percentage of households contained registered voters. The leaflets featured a large picture of a patriotic symbol, such as the Constitution or American soldiers hoisting the flag, described voting as a civic duty, gave the date of the upcoming election, and encouraged voters to participate. Leaflets did not list the polling location. This experiment involved 2,021 registered voters, far fewer than the Michigan study.

Figure 4-1. Sample Door Hanger

This door hanger was printed in three colors by the Michigan Democratic State Central Committee. It encourages both voting and support for Democratic candidates. Each door hanger indicates the voter's polling location and supplies a web address for further information.

Lessons Learned

The four lessons emerging from these studies are rated according to the system detailed in chapter 2: three stars are for findings that have received solid confirmation from several experiments, two stars are for more equivocal findings based on one or two experiments, and one star is for findings that are suggestive but not conclusive.

★★ *Partisan door hangers raise turnout by a small but statistically significant amount.* In both campaigns, for every sixty-six registered voters whose doors received hangers, one additional vote was produced.

★ *Partisan leaflets are about as effective in mobilizing frequent voters as they are in mobilizing infrequent voters.*

★ *Nonpartisan leaflets appear to generate votes at a rate of one vote per 200 residents receiving leaflets.* Although this rate appears to be somewhat smaller than for partisan mail, the statistical uncertainty associated with the nonpartisan experiment means that we cannot rule out the possibility that both campaigns were equally effective or that nonpartisan leaflets had no effect at all.

★ *Nonpartisan leaflets appear to be especially effective among voters who are "undeclared," that is, do not declare a party when registering to vote.* Because undeclared voters receive less communication from campaigns, leaflets might have greater salience for them. Consistent with this hypothesis, which was hinted in the nonpartisan study, the Michigan experiment found fairly strong effects among young voters, who are usually ignored by campaigns. Nevertheless, this hypothesis remains tentative.

Cost-Effectiveness

Once a campaign has secured a target list, leafleting involves two principal costs: the up-front cost of printing and the per hour cost of distribution. Assume that you are producing a partisan door hanger that tells each resident where to vote. The printing costs depend on the print volume, card size, paper stock, and number of colors. Suppose that you are planning to spend $0.08 on each leaflet (which is what the Michigan Democrats paid to print 100,000 door hangers).

Leafleteers are generally cheaper per hour than canvassers. Suppose you pay them $10 per hour with the expectation that they will drop leaflets at forty-five addresses per hour. Assuming that addresses contain an average of 1.5 voters, your leaflets reach 67.5 voters every hour. For every sixty-six voters contacted, one additional vote is generated. The labor costs of leafleting therefore come to approximately $10 per vote. The printing costs of the literature needed to produce one vote bring the total cost to approximately $13. If you are not printing in bulk, the cost per leaflet will rise. A more conservative figure, assuming $0.10 per leaflet, is $14 per vote. Adding the cost of supervision and infrastructure, of course, increases this figure.

Remember that this estimate of cost-effectiveness is based on just one partisan leafleting experiment. Until that study is replicated, it may be premature to draw any conclusions about the cost-effectiveness of leafleting.

Assessment and Conclusions

Leafleting operates on the principle that votes can be produced efficiently if leaflets have even a small impact on a large number of people. If your target population is large, leafleting may well be a cost-effective means of increasing turnout. However, if your jurisdiction is small enough to allow you to canvass the entire target population face-to-face, you should do so, because that will generate the most votes. Leafleting becomes an attractive option when vast numbers of voters otherwise would receive no contact from a face-to-face canvassing campaign.

Although leafleting experiments are relatively easy to conduct, they rarely have been conducted on a scale sufficient to produce informative results. Currently, the Michigan Democratic Party experiment towers above all other experiments of its kind, and further research is needed to determine whether partisan and nonpartisan messages have greater effects on certain subsets of the population, such as infrequent voters. The form and content of the leaflet are another aspect of the campaign that has only begun to receive experimental attention. Do door hangers increase turnout regardless of whether they instruct people about their polling location? Does it matter how people receive GOTV literature? Are leaflets different from direct mail in terms of their effects on voters? Or is direct mail just a leaflet delivered by the postal service?

CHAPTER FIVE

Direct Mail:
Postal Service as Campaign Staff

Just about every registered voter finds his or her mailbox filled with political mailings as election day approaches. So enormous is the volume of campaign mail that third-class and carrier route deliveries made by the U.S. Postal Service surge noticeably during the fourth quarter of even-numbered years.

Just as commercial direct mail enables vendors of all sizes to distribute advertising to large numbers of households, political direct mail permits a campaign of any size to contact large numbers of registered voters with a small investment of time and staff. Direct mail requires no recruiting of volunteers and no battles with inclement weather. With direct mail, much of the work can be done well in advance of the election. A few paid professionals can be employed to design, print, and distribute the mailings.

Although the administrative burdens of direct mail are minimal, the cost of preparation, printing, and postage can be considerable. At the high end of the market are direct mailings that are personalized for each voter. For example, political parties in states such as California send forms to voters enabling them to request absentee ballots. These forms have all of the necessary personal information already filled in; the addressee only needs to sign and mail the form. Another variation on this theme is direct mail that reminds the recipient of his or her polling location, perhaps even personalizing the campaign appeal based on the individual's demographic profile and place of residence. At the low end of the market are postcards with few colors, printed on relatively inexpensive paper stock. Regardless of the cost of preparing the mailer, postage must be paid for each piece of mail; for large mailings postage represents about half of the final cost. A typical direct mailing campaign will cost somewhere between $0.50 and $0.75 per piece. If you were to mail 25,000 voters three pieces of mail apiece, the final cost would be somewhere between $37,500 and $56,250. Cost per mailer drops when mailings are printed on a much larger scale or on small cardstock. Also, political parties receive a special discount on postage.

Is direct mail worth the cost? Most campaign managers seem to think it is. One veteran manager of state election campaigns, Darry Sragow, explains:

> Every Assembly race relies on mail if nothing else. Because certainly in urban districts, that's about the only medium we can employ practically. And we would want to do a minimum of five pieces of mail to anyone who has to be persuaded. It might be a couple of pieces of mail to reinforce the base, to motivate the base. But to someone who is genuinely in play, we would want to do at least five pieces . . . for the voter to know that the candidate exists. And then more to persuade the voter.[1]

In effect, the argument for direct mail is that a couple of mailings help to maintain the enthusiasm of a candidate's partisan supporters, perhaps even encouraging them to vote; moreover, a steady stream of direct mail helps to persuade swing voters.

Another line of argument on behalf of direct mail is that it reinforces the effectiveness of other campaign tactics, such as the use of phone banks. This was the strategy behind the NAACP National Voter Fund campaign in 2000. Given the overwhelmingly Democratic proclivities of African American voters, the campaign aimed to mobilize, not persuade. And to do this, a series of direct mailings dealing with issues such as racial profiling and hate crime were timed to coincide with televised advertisements and phone calls emphasizing similar themes. Even strictly nonpartisan efforts, such as the 2002 campaign of the National Association of Latino Elected Officials (NALEO) to mobilize Latino voters, sometimes combine direct mail with other GOTV tactics, such as live and prerecorded phone calls.

Skeptics question whether direct mail works (a view sometimes volunteered by persons selling other sorts of campaign services, such as robo calls). They argue that voters are inundated with junk mail and that at best they glance at campaign mail momentarily before putting it in the trash. The fact that these glances cost $0.50 apiece is cause for concern.

After summarizing the practical aspects of how a direct mail campaign is put together, this chapter attempts to determine whether direct mail raises voter turnout rates. Three types of direct mail are considered: strictly nonpartisan mail that seeks only to mobilize voters, issue advocacy mail that implicitly urges recipients to support a particular candidate, and partisan mail that openly endorses a particular candidate. The bottom line is that only strictly nonpartisan mail reliably increases voter turnout, and even then the effects tend to be modest. Mail from partisan and issue groups seems to have little effect on turnout, with the possible exception of mail sent to core partisan supporters. Even when it stimulates turnout, direct mail is usually more costly than other methods of producing votes, but it may serve the GOTV aims of campaigns that seek to reach a large and geographically dispersed audience whose phone numbers are unlisted or unreliable.

Organizing and Conducting a Direct Mail Campaign

When designing and implementing a GOTV direct mail program, keep the following rules of thumb in mind: plan ahead; get an accurate list of voters; make your mailings readable and eye-grabbing; line up your vendors; and learn the mechanics of sending bulk mail.

Plan ahead. Carefully plan the format and content of your mailing, determine your targeted voters, and set a production schedule. Almost invariably, you will encounter a holdup somewhere along the line—a delay at the printer, a direct mail company that is behind schedule, or a post office that sits on your mail. Several extra days or, better, a week should be built into the schedule to account for the unexpected.

Get an accurate list of voters. As discussed in previous chapters, you can obtain voter lists from a number of sources (see also box 5-1). Whatever source you choose, take time to check out its reputation for reliability and accuracy and make sure that the list it provides is as up-to-date as possible. Ask your list vendor to group voters by household rather than listing each voter individually. Addressing each mailer to all of the voters who are registered at a given address will save you the cost of sending multiple pieces of mail to one home.

Make your mailing pieces readable and eye-grabbing. Nonpartisan mail should use evocative language and images to emphasize the importance of

---

Box 5-1. Obtaining Mailing Lists

Registrars of voters, fortunately, keep fairly accurate records of current mailing addresses. If you get the most current list available prior to the election, expect less than 5 percent of mail sent to registered voters to be returned as undeliverable. If your target list comes from an interest group, such as a membership list, find out how recently the addresses were updated. One way to freshen a list is to pay a list vendor to check it against the national change of address registry. Some campaigns also send a postcard to everyone on the mailing list, as an inexpensive way to find out which addresses are no longer valid.

---

voting. For example, the mail used in New Haven featured images of Iwo Jima and reminded recipients that soldiers sacrificed their lives to preserve the right to vote. Partisan mail should try to communicate in words and images one or two simple take-home messages. Resist the temptation to put a lot of prose on your mailer, particularly on the outside. Bear in mind that most recipients will glance at the piece only momentarily en route to the trash can, so make sure that this book can be judged by its cover. If the budget permits, you should employ a professional graphic designer.

Although our experimental results suggest that a variety of reasonable direct mail appeals can be equally effective in mobilizing voters, those results apply to mailings that achieve a minimum threshold of professional competence. If your mailings do not reach this threshold, anything can happen, so take pains to ensure that they do not become an embarrassment. This means checking for spelling and punctuation errors, out-of-focus photos, and factual mistakes.

To avoid incurring unexpected costs, check with the post office to make sure that the piece envisioned is the proper size, weight, and format. Standard formats, with various folds, are 8.25" x 11" (one-fold card or postcard), 11" x 17", 11" x 22", or a 5.5" x 8.5" postcard.[2]

Line up your vendors. If possible, check out references on both the printer and the direct mail firm that you plan to hire. Be sure that they have the capability to handle a job of the size envisioned and that they enjoy a reputation for producing quality work and delivering it on schedule. The printer needs to understand the scope of the print job, including piece specifications, the number of copies of each piece, the paper stock, number of colors, and turnaround time. The direct mail firm also needs to receive a detailed outline of the artwork specifications, the number of pieces to be mailed, and mail- or drop-dates. Be sure to get written price quotes from any firm with which you do business.

Do-it-yourself direct mailers should learn the mechanics of bulk mail. Except for the occasional first-class letter, all of your pieces probably will be classified as bulk mail and sent through a bulk mail facility. Sending mail in bulk, as opposed to first class, will save at least 30 percent on postage costs. A direct mail firm will handle the bulk mail arrangements for you and almost certainly will include the bulk mail facility's service charges in its fee. If you do not hire a direct mail firm, you will have to handle all of the arrangements yourself. This means, first, obtaining a bulk mail permit, which you can do at the bulk mail division of your local post office. The post office will give you a permit number, and you should verify the exact wording and size for the bulk mail indicia that must be printed on each piece (the indicia typically reads "U.S. postage paid, city name, state, permit number"). The post office also will require you to fill out a form for each mailing that you send. Payment for postage costs is made directly to the post office.

Again, a direct mail firm will handle the details of delivering your pieces to the appropriate bulk mail facility. If you do not have a direct mail firm, you will have to do this yourself. You should ask the local post office how it wants the mail to be sorted. The mailbags should be red tagged (by you or the direct mail firm) to indicate that they contain political direct mail. By law, the post office is required to make political direct mail a priority over other direct mail. From there, the direct mail facility sorts and delivers the pieces of your mailing to the appropriate post offices. Mail carriers then deliver them to voters' homes.

The length of the process will vary. Some mail will move through the bulk mail facility and the post offices in one day and arrive at voters' homes within two to three days of its arrival at the bulk mail facility. Some post offices, however, move more slowly than others. And some post offices and bulk mail facilities get jammed with political mail during the days leading up to an election.

Try to determine the efficiency of the bulk mail facilities and post offices in your community. Be prepared to track your mail by establishing a relationship with a supervisor in the bulk mail facility and pushing to get the mail out in a timely manner. If your schedule is tight, visit the bulk mail facility in person when the mail arrives there. Following through can ensure that the mail is processed and distributed as quickly as possible. From there, you may need to contact each of the post offices that deliver to your targeted voters.

Experimental Research on Direct Mail

Hundreds of millions of dollars are spent on direct mail during each biennial election cycle. Much of this mail is intended to persuade, but some, like the National Voter Fund's 2000 direct mail campaign, is also intended to mobilize. The question is whether campaign mailings actually mobilize voters.

Political scientists have been studying the effects of direct mail on voter turnout since the 1920s. Harold Gosnell tested the effectiveness of nonpartisan GOTV appeals by mailing letters to Chicago residents encouraging them to vote.[3] He found that turnout increased 1 percent in the presidential election of 1924 and 9 percent in the municipal election of 1925. Of course, Gosnell's experiments were conducted in the days before computerized mailing lists made direct mail commonplace. One could well imagine that Chicagoans of the 1920s, who received mail only occasionally, might read Gosnell's missives with a level of curiosity that would be rare nowadays.

Since 1998 many experiments have sought to bring Gosnell's findings up to date. These studies have examined (1) strictly nonpartisan mail, whose only purpose was to encourage voter participation; (2) issue advocacy mail, which sought to rally voters behind an issue, implicitly encouraging them to vote for a particular candidate; and (3) partisan mail that clearly endorsed specific candidates. What follows is a brief chronology of these studies and a description of the electoral context in which they took place.

Nonpartisan Mail, 1998

During Connecticut's 1998 statewide election, we conducted a nonpartisan direct mail campaign in the city of New Haven.[4] We sought to learn three things about this direct mail campaign. First, how did the number of campaign mailings sent to voters affect their likelihood of showing up at the polls? Second, were the mobilizing effects of mail amplified when mail was used in conjunction with other mobilization tactics, such as phone calls? Lastly, did the content of these mailings affect voter turnout?

We began with a sample of 31,098 registered voters, of whom 5,064 received one mailing, 5,321 received two, and 5,200 received three. The control group of 15,513 received no mailings. The nonpartisan mailings were developed by professionals and contained one of three messages: (1) it is one's civic duty to vote, (2) voting is important because politicians pay special attention to the needs of neighborhoods that vote at high rates, and (3) the election is close, and every vote counts. Mailings were sent out at three intervals—fifteen days, thirteen days, and eight days before the election.

In this experiment, some of the recipients of direct mail also received encouragement to vote from door-to-door canvassers and commercial phone banks. This experimental design enabled us to assess whether mail amplified the effects of other voter mobilization techniques.

Nonpartisan Mail, 1999

Prior to the November 1999 municipal election we performed a follow-up experiment designed to measure the effect of sending a larger number of mailers.[5] In 1999 households were again randomly assigned either to a control group or to a treatment group receiving two, four, six, or eight pieces of nonpartisan mail. Mailings were sent approximately every two days, up until four days prior to the election (the groups receiving eight mailings were sent the first mailing eighteen days before the election, the groups receiving six mailings were sent the first mailing fourteen days before the election, and so forth).

Each of the treatment groups was randomly subdivided into two subgroups, with one group receiving mailings that emphasized the closeness of the elections and the other receiving mailings that emphasized civic duty. The point of this experiment was to test the proposition that messages have to be relevant in some way to the election at hand. There was nothing "close" about the 1999 mayoral election, which featured a Democratic incumbent running against a weak challenger in an overwhelmingly Democratic city. Would the "close election" appeal still work in this context?

Issue Advocacy, 2000

Prior to the 2000 elections, we conducted an experiment evaluating the direct mail campaign conducted by the NAACP National Voter Fund, which targeted African Americans and, where individuals' race could not be ascertained from the voter files, voters living in predominantly African American neighborhoods.[6] Before the experiment began, about one-third of the mailing list was sent a preliminary postcard to verify their address and two mailings dealing with the issue of hate crime. After these mailings went out, we randomized the distribution of subsequent mailings.

The GOTV mail that was the subject of this experimental analysis focused on the issue of discrimination. One mailer, for example, depicted a black motorist stopped by a white police officer brandishing a night-stick. The text surrounding the photo read, "Stopped again? Start voting." The text on the reverse side read:

> Getting stopped for "Driving While Black" is swerving out of control. We all know someone. Or we've had to deal with the frustration of it. And racial profiling hasn't just stopped there. Now's the time to do something about it. Vote. Let's start pulling the ballot lever and stop getting pulled over. Stop the madness. Vote. And get in the real driver's seat. Vote on Election Day, Tuesday November 7.

In certain states, voters who had not received an earlier mailing on hate crime were sent a different version of this mailing, which again implored them to "Stop the madness. Write Governor George W. Bush and tell him that we need hate crime legislation." Depending on the state being targeted, households were sent two or three pieces of GOTV mail. A parallel phone bank campaign struck similar themes, and mail and phone calls were timed to reinforce each other.

Partisan Mail, 1999

Our study of a 1999 mayoral campaign in a small Connecticut city involved 9,900 registered voters.[7] The direct mail campaign is of special interest because of its negative tone and the quantity of mail sent to targeted households. Three weeks before the election, the Democratic challenger's campaign began sending a series of nine pieces of mail to households chosen by the campaign on the basis of party and turnout history. The campaign also sent a single postcard to all households with at least one registered voter approximately one week before the election. We tested the effectiveness of the nine-piece campaign, not the postcard. From the Democrat's target list for the nine mailings, a control group was selected that received none of these mailings.

The Republican incumbent also sent direct mail, so registered voters received five Republican mailings in addition to the Democratic mailings. In effect, this experiment tested whether a dose of nine mailings affected turnout, given that recipients also received a postcard and five competing mailings.

This 1999 mayoral election was expected to be relatively close and was, by far, the most important and active contest on the ballot. The Democratic challenger targeted households that had at least one of the following: (a) a registered Democrat, (b) a registered "unaffiliated voter" who had voted in a recent election, or (c) a resident who had registered after November 1998.

The challenger waged what was considered to be a negative campaign. He attacked the incumbent as an incompetent, wasteful manager who was looking out for special interests. As is common in such campaigns, the negative mailings were sandwiched between more positive mailings. The first and last pieces provided upbeat assessments of the sponsoring candidate, presumably with the intention of restoring good feelings about the candidate and inspiring support.

Another partisan mail experiment took place in New Jersey, which held state legislative elections in 1999. New Jersey elects two state assembly members from each district. In this partisan campaign, an incumbent New Jersey state legislator ran what amounted to a joint campaign with another Democratic incumbent from the same district.

The assembly campaign targeted three groups with somewhat different mail campaigns. Households containing frequently voting Democrats, or "prime Democrats," received four mailings. Other Democrats and Independents received six pieces of mail. The Republicans and infrequently voting Independents received either four or six mailings. From each group a selected control group received no mailings from this campaign. Taken together, the New Jersey partisan mail experiments assigned approximately 5,000 voters to the control group and 30,000 to the treatment group. This protocol allowed us to evaluate whether certain potential voting groups were more influenced by direct mail than others.

Partisan Mail, 2000

Two experiments involved the reelection campaign of a Republican incumbent member of Congress.[8] The primary election featured a credible challenger; the general election was won decisively. In order to study the effects of direct mail sent in advance of the primary election, random-ization was performed at the precinct level. Of the precincts that were targeted for a two-piece direct mail campaign, five were placed in a con-trol group that received no mail. The general election campaign targeted households other than those in which all members were Democrats who voted in primaries. "Prime Republicans," defined as those who vote reg-ularly in primary elections, received one mailing, other Republicans received two, and non-Republicans received three.

Nonpartisan Mail, 2002

Two nonpartisan mobilization campaigns targeting ethnic minorities tested the effects of direct mail in 2002. Janelle Wong of the University of Southern California assessed the effects of a single mailing aimed at Los Angeles County voters with Chinese, Indian, Japanese, Korean, and Filipino surnames.[9] A total of 3,232 voters were sent mail, with 8,726 assigned to a control group. The mailing sent to Chinese Americans was bilingual; all other recipients received English-language mail.

In a study designed by Ricardo Ramírez of the University of Southern California, NALEO sent two to four pieces of mail targeting registered voters with Latino surnames in Denver, Houston, Los Angeles County, Orange County, New Mexico, and New York.[10] The foldout mailings were all bilingual and featured high-quality color graphics. The size of this experiment was very large, with roughly 300,000 voters sent mail and another 60,000 relegated to a control group. Furthermore, the experiment examined whether the effectiveness of mail varied depending on whether it was paired with live or prerecorded phone calls.

Lessons Learned

The four lessons emerging from these studies are rated according to the system detailed in chapter 2: three stars are for findings that have received solid confirmation from several experiments, two stars are for more equivocal findings based on one or two experiments, and one star is for findings that are suggestive but not conclusive.

★★ *Nonpartisan direct mail increases turnout by a rate of one additional voter for every 200 recipients.* Since the average mailing address on a voter registration list contains 1.5 registered voters, this rate translates into one additional vote for every 133 pieces of mail. A word of caution is in order, however. The New Haven experiments in 1998 and 1999 showed that nonpartisan direct mail had significantly positive effects, a finding bolstered by the Asian American mailing experiment in 2002. However, the NALEO experiment in 2002 did not generate an increase in turnout. The NALEO experiment is sufficiently large to rule out chance as an explanation. Thus the one-for-133 finding should be considered an optimistic estimate.

★ *The mobilizing effects of nonpartisan direct mail appear to taper off after six mailings per address.* The 1999 nonpartisan mailing campaign in New Haven found that turnout among those sent civic duty appeals was highest among those who received six mailings as opposed to none, two, four, or eight.

★★ *The precise content of nonpartisan mail does not seem to matter, so long as the message is not ridiculous.* None of the nonpartisan messages stood out as particularly effective, but one message was noteworthy for its ineffectiveness. Telling people to vote because one vote can make a difference is wholly ineffective when the election is expected to be a blowout. This finding implies that at least some people are paying attention to content.

★ *Interest group mail expressing opposition to a candidate shows little indication of mobilizing voters, especially voters who had earlier been exposed to similar direct mail communication.* The NAACP National Voter Fund mail experiment showed a slight increase in voter turnout among those in the treatment group who received no mail before the experiment began. Those who had previously received mail were unmoved by mail sent toward the end of the campaign. This pattern is consistent with the diminishing returns noted earlier.

★★ *Partisan mail appears to have a mobilizing effect when sent to frequent voters of the same party.* Partisan mail appears to "motivate the base." Both the Democratic mail sent by state assembly candidates and the Republican mail sent by a congressional candidate had the greatest impact on the "prime" partisan supporters. Also consistent with this interpretation is the fact that partisan mail appears to be especially effective at mobilizing voters in party primary elections.

★★ *Partisan mail has little mobilizing effect on infrequent voters or randomly selected members of a registration list.* Neither Democratic nor

Republican mail in the two experimental campaigns had any appreciable effect on voters other than prime supporters. Direct mail campaigns that focus on so-called swing voters—those without strong partisan ties—may be able to persuade but should not expect to mobilize.

★ *Partisan mail campaigns that have a sharp negative tone may diminish turnout slightly.*

★★ *There is no evidence of synergy between mail and other GOTV tactics.* For example, in the 1998 New Haven experiment, there is no indication that mail worked better among those who were called or visited at their doorstep. In the NAACP National Voter Fund and NALEO studies, mail was no more effective among those who received phone calls.

Cost-Effectiveness

A generous assessment of the effects of nonpartisan mail suggests that it increases turnout by one vote for every 200 people who are sent a piece of mail. The typical address on a voter registration file contains 1.5 voters on average, so if mail is addressed to all voters at a household, voter turnout increases by one vote for every 133 pieces of mail. Since the effects of mail seem to level out after about six mailings, let us suppose that no more than six pieces of mail are sent to each household. At $0.75 per piece of mail, it takes $100 of mail to produce one additional vote. At $0.50 per piece of mail, this figure drops to $67 per vote. This estimate makes direct mail substantially more expensive than other nonpartisan GOTV tactics, such as door-to-door canvassing or, as we show in the next chapter, certain types of volunteer phone banks.

The calculation of cost-efficiency is somewhat different in the case of partisan campaigns. Of course, partisan campaigns could simply send out nonpartisan mail to those they hope to mobilize, but the typical partisan campaign makes appeals on behalf of a candidate. When directed at the party's core supporters, mail does raise turnout. In the New Jersey assembly race, four mailings aimed at "prime Democrats" raised their turnout from 63.7 to 65.6 percent. In the Pennsylvania general election campaign for Congress, a single mailer aimed at "prime Republicans" raised turnout from 89.0 percent to 90.6 percent. Taken together, these two experiments imply that one vote is produced for every 118 mailings sent. At this rate, if it costs $0.50 to send a mailing to a household, each additional vote costs $59. This figure is subject to a good deal of statistical uncertainty, but it appears that when mobilizing core supporters, partisan mail is about as effective as nonpartisan mail.

When partisan direct mail is either negative in tone or directed toward nonprime partisans, this GOTV tactic looks bleak from the standpoint of cost-efficiency. The New Jersey state assembly campaign that sent six mailings to households consisting primarily of Independents and Democrats who vote infrequently had no effect on turnout (turnout rates were 54.2 percent for both treatment and control groups). The assembly mailings to a random sample of the list of registered voters boosted turnout from 23.1 percent in the control group to 23.5 percent among those receiving four mailings and 24.1 percent among those receiving six. In this case, each piece of mail boosted turnout at a rate of approximately $200 per vote. Partisan mail may, of course, serve other purposes, such as building name recognition and persuading voters of a candidate's merits. But don't pin your hopes on mobilizing the typical voter with partisan mail.

Even demobilizing strategies may be hard to justify on cost-effectiveness grounds. It is sometimes argued that campaigns send negative mail in the hopes of encouraging their partisan opponents to stay home. We find some support for the notion that negative campaigns depress turnout, but a few caveats are in order. First, the effect is small and, despite the large number of people involved in that experiment, not statistically robust. Second, even if demobilization "works," it is important to bear in mind that the mayoral campaign targeted households that were thought to contain voters who would be sympathetic to the Democratic candidate. It turns out that the demobilization effect was as strong among registered Democrats as it was for other targets of the mail. Third, even if the demobilization effect had scared off only voters who would have voted for the opposing candidate, the fact that nine pieces of mail lowered turnout by just 1 percentage point means that a demobilization strategy cannot be considered cost-effective. Nine mailings cost approximately $4.50 per household. Sending this regimen of mail out to sixty-seven households (containing 100 voters) diminished turnout at a cost of $300 per vote.

Assessment and Conclusions

Direct mail is expensive, and its capacity to mobilize voters is typically rather limited. Nevertheless, direct mail makes sense for certain types of campaigns. If the campaign lacks the people power needed to distribute door hangers or the time to manage these ground efforts, direct mail is a sensible alternative. Direct mail has the further advantage of allowing centralized control of very large campaigns, which explains why national organizations turn to direct mail when targeting hundreds of thousands of voters. Our results indicate that direct mail does nudge voter turnout upward, but it is important to be realistic about what to expect from such a campaign. The *largest* effect we have seen from a partisan mail campaign is a 1.9 percentage-point increase in turnout at the individual level.

Finally, it should be stressed that we have focused exclusively on voter mobilization. Mail that advocates on behalf of a candidate or issue may win votes through persuasion, not mobilization. Partisan campaigns may justify the use of direct mail on the grounds that it changes *how* people will vote even if it does not change *whether* people vote. It turns out, incidentally, that experiments designed to detect these persuasive effects have found mixed results, but that is a story for another book.

CHAPTER SIX

Phone Banks:
Politics Meets Telemarketing

You know them, you hate them: unsolicited telephone calls, typically occurring while you are preparing or eating dinner, bathing the kids, or settling down to relax for the evening. Phone calls from survey takers, telemarketers, or even campaign volunteers are rarely welcome. Nevertheless, every election year vast quantities of time and money are devoted to get-out-the-vote phone calls, some by paid professional callers, some by volunteers and paid campaign staff, and some by prerecorded messages. Despite people's aversion to these calls, they must mobilize voters, right? Yes . . . and no.

In this chapter, we discuss the various ways in which campaigns use the telephone in an attempt to mobilize voters. After laying out the steps required to orchestrate phone canvassing, we evaluate the experimental evidence about the effectiveness of volunteer phone banks, commercial phone banks, and prerecorded messages.

Our findings suggest that phone banks work to the extent that they establish an authentic personal connection with voters. Prerecorded messages seem ineffective. Commercial phone banks that plow through get-out-the-vote scripts at a rapid pace and with little conviction do little to increase turnout. Phone banks staffed by enthusiastic volunteers typically are effective in raising turnout, although the vagaries of organizing volunteers for a sustained period of time often limit the number of people who can be reached in this manner. When commercial phone banks are carefully coached—and paid a premium to slow their callers down—they can be as effective as volunteer phone banks. Managing a phone bank campaign therefore requires attention not only to the mechanics of making a lot of calls but also to the quality of each call.

Types of Phone Campaigns

There are five basic requirements for a telephone canvassing campaign: staff to make calls, several phone lines, a central location where callers can be supervised, a target list of potential voters (preferably with an up-to-date list of phone numbers), and a script that callers read or paraphrase (see box 6-1). How these ingredients are put together depends on whether the phone bank in question is making prerecorded or live calls and, if the latter, whether the calls are made by campaign activists, paid staff, or professionals hired by a commercial phone bank. Before evaluating the performance of each type of phone bank, we first describe some of the practical aspects of each type of operation.

Professional Phone Banks

With the advent of commercial telemarketing firms, the technology used to conduct large-scale calling campaigns has become commonplace. Equipped with automatic dialers and computer-assisted interviewing technology, a large number of national and regional firms are capable of contacting hundreds of thousands of households each day. Commercial phone banks, moreover, require relatively little lead time; with the script and target list in hand, a telemarketing firm typically requires only a matter of hours before phone canvassing can get under way. The capacity to generate large numbers of calls with little lead time gives phone banks an edge over other GOTV tactics during the waning days of a campaign. That is why at the end of a campaign the remaining contents of the war chest are often dumped into a commercial phone bank.

Even if you plan to conduct your calls during the last weekend before election day, make time beforehand to shop around and develop a thoughtful and well-executed phone campaign. Phone banks offer a wide array of pricing options, reflecting at least in part the fact that their callers and training practices vary in quality. As we show in this chapter, the quality of the calls plays a crucial role in determining whether or not they actually generate votes.

The typical campaign has little use for the data that are collected by telemarketing firms, but you should request this information anyway for accounting purposes. Unless you are a regular customer, you will have to

---

Box 6-1. Building a Targeted Phone List

Public voter files and even commercially distributed voter lists are often loaded with outdated phone numbers. Regardless of how you develop your list, if you are conducting a phone bank and have the resources, you probably should hire a phone-matching firm to match names with updated phone numbers or have the list vendor do this for you. When shopping for a firm, find out how recently the phone numbers were updated for your target jurisdiction. To keep the cost of matching down, pare down your list to the persons you intend to call. Lastly, if your target list is very small, and you have the time, patience, and volunteers to do so, look up phone numbers the old-fashioned way, using local directories.

---

pay phone banks a deposit up-front, usually based on a setup fee and an estimated cost per completion. Be sure that you have a clear understanding of what counts as a completion before signing the contract and, after the calls have been completed, examine the records of whether and how each target name was contacted in order to ensure that the charges are fair. This guards against the possibility that phone banks will rely on an overly generous definition of what counts as a contact.

Put your own name (and the names of relatives and campaign workers who agree to be guinea pigs) onto the target list, so that you can track what the phone bank is doing. You also should take advantage of one of the high-tech perks of using a commercial phone bank, namely, the ability to listen in on GOTV calls. Monitoring the calls, especially early in the calling campaign, can be critical to your quality control efforts. It is not unusual to encounter a particular caller who is misreading the message, going too fast, or speaking with an accent that your target audience will find jarring. Monitoring calls also gives you an opportunity to discover whether the phone bank is charging you for "break-offs," that is, calls in which the recipient hangs up after a few seconds.

Robo Calls

A second approach to telephone canvassing is to contact voters with a prerecorded message known as a robo call. The recorded message may be provided directly by the candidate, by a member of the candidate's family, or by a prominent local or national figure endorsing the candidate. Depending on the amount of demographic information that is available for individual voters, you can design different messages for different groups—one for young people, another for women, still another for Latinos.

The advantages of robo calling are that the calls are consistent in quality, relatively inexpensive, and easy to produce on short notice. They are designed as much for answering machines as for live respondents. Those who tout their virtues frequently recount anecdotes of voters who come home from work only to discover a memorable message on their answering machine from Bill Clinton, Barbara Bush, or LL Cool J.

Robo calls, like live calls, require a list of phone numbers, but once these fixed costs have been paid, the unit costs of robo calling are much lower. Robo calls are usually priced in the neighborhood of $0.05 apiece, which is roughly one-tenth the cost of live calls. (Again, be sure that you are being charged per completion not per attempt.) Thus establishing some minimal level of name recognition among 100,000 households would cost just $5,000. Getting out votes, however, is a more difficult task than getting your name into circulation, so the key question is whether robo calls actually increase recipients' likelihood of going to the polls.

Volunteer Phone Banks

A third option is to organize a calling effort yourself. A homegrown phone bank may be staffed by activists supporting your campaign, by paid staff, or by a combination of the two. For the purposes of explaining how a phone bank operation is put together, we lump activists and paid volunteers together under the heading "volunteers," but bear in mind that these two types of workers are very different. It should be clear by the end of this chapter that activists—those who genuinely believe in the cause embodied by your campaign—are much more effective than people who walk in off the street in search of a job.

Recruitment

Your first task is to recruit callers. Intuition suggests, and our research confirms, that callers who establish credibility and rapport have the greatest success in turning out voters via the telephone. Indeed, the principal advantage of organizing a volunteer phone bank is that the callers will convey an authentic sense of enthusiasm and commitment. The ease with which such callers can be found will depend on the nature of your campaign and those active within it. An articulate and motivated group of callers can move mountains; their evil twins (the ones who fail to show up, show up late, or accomplish little once they arrive) can be an expensive and demoralizing headache.

It is important to recruit more volunteers than you will actually need, because many who promise to appear will not show up on calling day. Twice the number needed is a reasonable rule of thumb. Providing some enticement for callers can be useful. Depending on the pool of volunteers and the time of day that the phone bank operates, donuts and coffee beforehand or a pizza party afterward are options. As mentioned in the chapter on door-to-door canvassing, it is usually cheaper—and perhaps wiser, from the standpoint of finances and morale—to pay workers with food and drink than with hourly wages.

Location

In principle, you can coordinate a phone bank in a decentralized manner, with callers working from home. Although less expensive, this type of arrangement creates potentially serious supervisory problems. Even if the callers are doing their work, you cannot monitor whether they are staying "on message" and conveying the proper tone. For this reason, most campaigns prefer to have phone bank volunteers make their calls from a central location. In assessing alternative sites, factors that must be taken into consideration include acoustics, physical layout (caller privacy has advantages, but so does a layout in which callers can be seen by one another and by the organizers), and facilities such as parking, restrooms, and perhaps even a refrigerator or soda machine. Obviously, geographic location will loom large if your campaign plans to make long-distance calls.

Work Shifts and Phone Capacity

After identifying your labor pool and workplace, try to determine how many calls you can expect to complete in the days remaining in the campaign. Our experience suggests that with an up-to-date list of phone numbers and a chatty script, a competent caller will complete eight calls per hour with the intended targets and leave another eight messages with the targets' housemate. You can use this figure to calculate the number of person-hours that will be required in order to meet your objectives. For example, if you seek to complete 8,000 calls and leave 8,000 messages, your labor pool will need to furnish 1,000 person-hours. If the calls will be made on weekday evenings from 5:00 p.m. to 9:00 p.m. and on weekends from 9:00 a.m to 6:00 p.m., a single phone line used to full capacity will generate thirty-eight hours of calls per week. If the calls will be made over two weeks, you will need fourteen phone lines.

Of course, the supply of labor may not cooperate with these simple calculations. Phone bank organizers often fail to plan for surges in the number of canvassers who report for duty. A GOTV phone drive that we studied in Houston, for example, foundered because the phone bank attracted more than 200 volunteers for only twelve phones. The inevitable outcome was disappointment for the organizers and frustration for the volunteers. If your campaign has the potential to snowball into something large, it is best to err on the side of having too many phones (or have ready access to cell phones). Sometimes a large supportive business will permit volunteers to make their calls from its offices after hours. Just remind your callers not to leave empty soda bottles on the mahogany furniture.

Training

Although volunteers should devote as much time as possible to the central task of contacting voters, it is important to begin your phone drive (and to welcome each new group of volunteers) with a brief training session on how to deal with a variety of contingencies. Should callers leave messages on answering machine or voice mail? How should they respond to voters who are hostile to the candidate or to the GOTV effort? How important is it for callers to stay on script? Should they speak only with the person or persons named on a calling sheet, or should they give their pitch to anyone who answers the phone? How should they respond to voters who request more information about the campaign or who ask to be called back at another time? And what information should callers record on the calling sheets as they place calls?

With regard to this last question, you may wish to have callers record not just the names they contact but also those who are not at home, those for whom recorded messages were left, and invalid telephone numbers or numbers that did not correspond to the voter named on the list. This information will enable you to track the progress of the GOTV effort and to direct volunteers to make a second or third attempt if time permits. The training session should provide volunteers with answers to all of these questions. A consistent written protocol to cover all likely situations, distributed and carefully explained to volunteers, will make things easier for them and will minimize unforeseen problems. Provide all callers with a printed instruction sheet and a copy of the script to keep near the phone. This is especially important for volunteers who arrive late and miss some of the training.

Prepare a Script

The final task of the planning process is to script the pitch that volunteers will deliver to the voters they contact. Whether your script should be formal or more casual will depend on the specific goals of the phone drive, the characteristics of targeted voters, and the enthusiasm of the volunteers. Callers should be instructed on whether to adopt a crisp professional tone or to engage in a more conversational and unstructured discussion. Using a standardized script has advantages. A reasonable degree of consistency among your callers is guaranteed, and less supervision is required. Volunteers, especially those without past experience with phone banks, will have the psychological comfort of clearly understanding what is expected of them. Nonetheless, our research suggests that more conversational calls—perhaps because they are unhurried and responsive to the reactions of the recipient—tend to have a greater impact on voters than tightly scripted calls.

Confirm All Details

To protect against last-minute glitches, it is advisable to confirm all the details about a week before the phone drive is to begin. Items to check include the continued availability of the calling center, the required number of phones, adequate parking, and amenities for callers.

Even if your campaign is blessed with experienced and motivated volunteers, it is always advisable to call volunteers ahead of time to remind each of them of their commitment to participate. If the phone drive is being conducted on several successive evenings, you might assign one volunteer each evening to spend a few minutes contacting those who are signed up for the next day, or you could place these calls yourself. Despite your best efforts to remind and encourage volunteers, however, expect less than 100 percent attendance, even among the people who repeatedly promise to show up.

Supervision and Assistance during the Phone Drive

Campaign staff or a volunteer coordinator should be present on-site throughout the phone drive. If you are calling from several locations, each requires a supervisor. Volunteers may have questions or problems, need encouragement, drift off-message, or waste time musing about the range of possible toppings that could embellish the next pizza. Supervision will ensure that volunteers stay on task and that the phone bank proceeds smoothly. Good training will minimize the amount of oversight required.

Experimental Research on Telephone Calling

More than a dozen recent experiments have assessed whether phone calls mobilize voters. First, we consider the mobilizing effects of robo calls, both partisan and nonpartisan. Second, we summarize a series of experiments on the mobilizing effects of commercial phone banks. Finally, we discuss the rich array of volunteer phone banks that have been subjected to experimental evaluation.

Robo Calls: No Discernible Effect on Turnout

In a study conducted in Seattle in November 2001, a nonpartisan group hired a robo call vendor to place 10,000 calls with a recorded message from the local registrar of voters reminding citizens to vote in the next day's municipal elections. The turnout rate among those who were called was no higher than that of the control group. This pattern held for those who voted in person as well as those who voted absentee. Of course, it could be argued that the registrar of voters lacked the pizzazz of a movie star or famous politician. But the Seattle experiment nonetheless shows that reminders to vote do not in and of themselves raise turnout rates. The significance of this point should not be underestimated. "Forgetting" election day is not why registered voters fail to cast ballots. Low voter turnout reflects low motivation, not amnesia.

As for celebrity robo calls, two experimental studies were conducted by organizations trying to mobilize particular ethnic groups. The NAACP National Voter Fund used celebrity robo calls in its 2000 GOTV campaign. Here, two robo calls, one from Bill Clinton and the other from radio personality Tom Joyner, were combined with four live calls from a commercial phone bank staffed by African American callers. Millions of calls were made, but the overall effect of the phone campaign was only slightly positive, suggesting that neither live nor robo calls had much effect.

Unlike the National Voter Fund campaign, which combined robo calls with live calls, the National Association of Latino Elected Officials made only robo calls to mobilize Latino voters in five states. Again, two calls were placed to each voter, one from a Spanish-language-television anchorwoman and another from a local radio or television celebrity. Both messages were conveyed in Spanish (except in one region, where one of the calls was in English). Robo calls again appeared to have a miniscule effect on turnout. Approximately one vote was produced for every 2,000 voters contacted either directly or through a recording on their answering machine. Despite the enormous size of this experiment, which involved more than 250,000 people in the treatment group and 100,000 in the control group, the mobilizing effects of robo calls were so weak that they could not be distinguished statistically from zero.

The results suggest that robo calls have a minimal effect on turnout. From the standpoint of cost-efficiency, even a tiny positive effect might make this inexpensive technology worthwhile. Thus far, however, experimenters have yet to isolate this tiny positive effect. Robo calls might help you to stretch your resources in ways that allow you to contact the maximum number of people, but don't expect to move them very much, if at all.

Commercial Phone Banks

Earlier, we mentioned the weak positive effects of the NAACP National Voter Fund's phone bank effort, which combined robo and live calls. It turns out that weak effects are the rule rather than the exception for commercial phone banks. In 1998 we conducted two nonpartisan campaigns using a single commercial phone bank.[1] The smaller of the two campaigns was conducted in New Haven; a much larger study was conducted in neighboring West Haven. In both experiments, the group receiving phone calls voted at rates that were no greater than the control group receiving no calls. None of the three scripts—one stressing civic duty, another, neighborhood solidarity, and a third, the possibility of deciding a close election—had any appreciable impact.

Curious as to whether this result was due to the failings of a single phone bank, we replicated the 1998 experiments on a grand scale in 2002.[2] Congressional districts in Iowa and Michigan were divided into two categories, depending on whether they featured competitive or uncompetitive races. Within each category, 15,000 randomly selected individuals at distinct addresses were assigned to be called by one of two commercial phone banks, each delivering the same nonpartisan message. Thus 60,000 people in all were called in the treatment group, and more than 1 million names were placed in the control group. In the 2002 study, the treatment effects were just barely on the positive side of zero. Taken at face value, the results suggest that these phone banks were mobilizing one additional voter for every 280 people they spoke with, but the effects were not statistically distinguishable from zero. The enormous samples in these experiments mean that we can decisively rule out the possibility that these commercial phone banks had big effects.

John McNulty of University of California, Berkeley conducted an experiment examining the effects of advocacy calls made by a campaign seeking to defeat a municipal ballot measure in San Francisco.[3] Close to 30,000 calls (about half resulting in successful contact) were made by a commercial phone center located in the Midwest. The script was very brief:

Hello [name], I'm calling on behalf of the Coalition for San Francisco Neighborhoods, reminding you to oppose Proposition D. Proposition D is a risky scheme that allows the PUC [Public Utility Commission] to issue revenue bonds without voter approval. These bonds would be paid back through higher utility rates. Can we count on you to join us in opposing Proposition D next Tuesday?

Consistent with other findings concerning the delivery of brief scripts by commercial phone banks, one vote was produced for every 200 successful contacts.

Before giving up on commercial phone banks, we must consider the possibility that the effectiveness of these calls hinges on the manner in which they are delivered. Having eavesdropped on many hours of commercial phone canvassing, we know that many callers rush through the scripts. Their mechanical style conveys little enthusiasm about voting. These callers, who can forge through fifty or so completed calls per hour, behave much as one would expect given the incentives of piecework and the eagerness of supervisors to move on to the next calling campaign.

In 2002 we evaluated a youth-oriented voter mobilization campaign in which a commercial phone bank was paid top dollar to deliver its GOTV appeal in a chatty and unhurried manner.[4] The script required the reader to pause for questions and to invite respondents to visit a website in order to learn more about their polling location. A good deal of coaching ensured that this appeal was read at the proper speed. Between one and four calls were made to randomly selected subgroups of young people over the four-week period leading up to election day. The phone bank kept records of each person they contacted, so that when respondents were contacted a second time, the script took notice of the fact that the previous conversation was being resumed. Because the experiment was very large and spread over more than a dozen regions, the results provide an unusually nuanced assessment of whether and when calls are most effective.

The bottom line is that these calls produced a substantial and statistically significant increase in voter turnout in the target group, but only among those called during the final week of the campaign. In other words, calls made during the first three weeks of a month-long GOTV campaign had no apparent effect on voter turnout. Calls made during the last week produced one vote for every twenty contacts. If we smooth the results statistically on the theory that calls become gradually more effective as election day approaches, it appears that calls during the last week produced one vote for every thirty contacts. Any way you look at it, these are big effects.

This phone bank proved influential among a wide demographic array of voters. Both African American voters in North Carolina and whites in Minneapolis turned out at higher rates as a result of these calls. Lest you think that young people happen to be more susceptible to GOTV calls, the Iowa and Michigan studies, which used standard commercial phone banks, showed no effects among young people.

As further proof that a carefully supervised phone bank campaign can work, another commercial phone bank was trained by Youth Vote staff in Denver (see box 6-2). An even lengthier script was prepared for the callers, who were selected on the basis of age, told about Youth Vote's mission, and given Youth Vote buttons to wear while making calls. Youth Vote staff sat with the callers on site as they made their calls, to ensure the quality of the operation. When the election was over, turnout figures showed this phone bank to be quite successful, increasing turnout by one voter for every eighteen people contacted.

It appears that quality of the phone call makes all the difference.

Volunteer Phone Banks

The relaxed, authentic style of most volunteer phone banks provides the right ingredients for success. A wealth of experimental evidence, however, cautions that volunteer phone banks are often, but not always, effective. For example, in the weeks leading up to the November 2000 elections, the Youth Vote coalition of nonpartisan organizations targeting young voters had mixed success in generating votes. Of the four sites

Box 6-2. A "Conversational" Youth Vote 2002 Script

Hi [first name], my name is [your full name], and I'm calling on behalf of the Youth Vote Coalition [pronounce slowly and clearly as it is hard for many people to understand "Youth Vote" the first time they hear it]. This is not a sales call, and we are not affiliated with any particular political party or candidate. Youth Vote is a national nonprofit, nonpartisan organization composed of diverse groups all working together to increase voter turnout among eighteen- to thirty-year-olds.

The reason we are contacting you is to thank you for registering to vote. You have taken the first crucial step in giving yourself the power to make your voice heard in our democracy. However, even more important than that is the fact that you actually DO vote on election day. This year's Senate race in Colorado is especially important and could have national implications in determining the balance of power in Congress. It is expected that less than 500 votes may determine the outcome of this race. Your vote can make a difference. Thus we encourage you to take the time to vote in the upcoming election on TUESDAY, NOVEMBER 5th between the hours of 7 a.m. and 7 p.m.

Have you received your voter registration card in the mail?

[If yes:] OK, that tells you where your polling location is. But just so you know, your polling location is at [name of place and address]. Again, you can vote between the hours of 7 a.m. and 7 p.m. and will need to show your voter registration card and/or a government-issued picture ID. Lastly, we would like to provide you with a toll-free phone number and websites for obtaining nonpartisan information on the candidates and issues in your area. The number is 1-888-Vote-Smart (1-888-868-3762), and the websites are www.vote-smart.org (make sure you say vote-dash-smart.org) and www.youthvote.org.

Well [person's first name], I'd like to thank you for your time. Again, remember to mark your calendar to vote on Tuesday, November 5th, and encourage your friends and family to vote, too. Have a good evening.

in the experiment, two showed large effects (Albany and Stony Brook), and two showed weak effects (Boulder and Eugene). Overall, one vote was generated for every twenty-two contacts. When Youth Vote repeated this experiment in 2001, this time targeting voters of all ages, the effects were weaker but still positive.

Finally, in 2002, the volunteer phone banks were pitted against the commercial phone bank described above in an effort to figure out which approach produced more young votes. This time, the volunteer phone banks were given very ambitious goals—to contact thousands or even tens of thousands of voters. Many sites got a late start in organizing their campaigns and were forced to turn to paid staff, in some cases from temporary employment agencies. Turnover among callers was high, and supervisory staff was stretched thin by responsibilities other than the phone bank. This meant that local sites frequently relied on callers with minimal training. The net result was a disappointment: the local phone banks increased turnout at a rate of one voter for every 59 calls.

The importance of enthusiasm and training is further illustrated by three successful efforts in 2002. A partisan GOTV campaign funded by the Michigan Democratic Party attempted to contact 10,550 registered voters between the ages of eighteen and thirty-five and completed calls with 5,319 of them. The net effect was to raise turnout significantly among those contacted: one additional vote was produced for every twenty-nine people contacted.[5] NALEO's local phone bank campaign, which was directed toward Latino registered voters in Los Angeles and Orange counties, raised turnout significantly among those contacted, producing one vote for every twenty-two contacts.[6] A nonpartisan phone bank in Los Angeles County, organized by University of Southern California professor Janelle Wong, targeted ethnic Chinese voters and raised turnout significantly.[7]

Again, this is not to say that volunteer phone banks staffed by enthusiastic callers are a surefire success. Several of the other Asian groups that Wong targeted in Los Angeles County were unmoved by the GOTV appeal. It may be that the brevity of her voting reminders and the lack of ethnic appeal robbed the scripts of some of their impact (see boxes 6-3 and 6-4 for sample scripts).

Overall, volunteer phone banks have a fairly good track record of mobilizing those whom they contact. The rule of thumb that emerges from our review of this literature is that one additional voter is produced for every thirty-five contacts (or twenty-eight contacts per vote if phone banks with paid staff are excluded from the category of volunteer phone

Box 6-3. Ethnic Mobilization Script

The National Association of Latino Elected Officials used the following script, in English or Spanish, depending on the language spoken by the respondent:

Good evening, my name is [your name]. I'm calling on behalf of NALEO. I am calling to remind you that the upcoming election will be held on Tuesday, November 5th. Your vote will help build a stronger community. Do you plan to vote on Tuesday, November 5th?

[If the response is yes:] Your participation in the upcoming election means better schools, better jobs, and safer neighborhoods. To keep our community growing, we have to vote. Don't forget to vote in the upcoming election on Tuesday, November 5th. The polls will be open from 7 a.m. to 8 p.m. Thank you and have a good evening.

[If the response is no:] Your vote is very important in the upcoming election. Your vote can ensure better schools, better jobs, and safer neighborhoods. To keep our community growing, we must vote. NALEO encourages you to vote in the upcoming election on Tuesday, November 5th. The polls will be open from 7 a.m. to 8 p.m. Thank you and have a good evening.

Box 6-4. Example of a Reminder Script

Janelle Wong of the University of Southern California organized a multilingual phone bank in Los Angeles that made nonpartisan turnout appeals to 1,598 registered voters with Chinese, Japanese, Korean, Indian, and Filipino surnames. The script was very brief, consisting of little more than a reminder to vote.

Hi. May I please speak to Mr./Mrs./Ms. [last name or full name]? My name is [your name], and I'm a student at USC. I'm calling from CAUSE-Vision21. I'm not trying to sell you anything. I just wanted to call and remind you to vote on Tuesday, November 5. If you have any questions about voting, you can call this hotline: 888-809-3888.

banks). The real question for volunteer phone banks is not whether they work under optimal conditions but rather whether they can achieve a sufficient volume of calls to make a difference. It is the rare volunteer phone bank that can complete the 30,000 calls needed to generate 1,000 votes. The experience of Youth Vote in 2002 suggests that striving to expand the quantity of calls can jeopardize their quality.

Lessons Learned

The lessons emerging from these studies are rated according to the system detailed in chapter 2: three stars are for findings that have received solid confirmation from several experiments, two stars are for more equivocal findings based on one or two experiments, and one star is for findings that are suggestive but not conclusive.

★★ *Robo calls have very weak effects on voter turnout.* Thus far, none of the experiments using robo calls has been able to distinguish their effects from zero. Our best guess places the vote production rate somewhere in the neighborhood of one vote per 2,000 contacts, but given the shaky state of the evidence, robo calls may have no effect at all. If you are attempting to mobilize voters in a constituency with millions of people and willing to gamble that robo calls do work, they may be a cost-effective option, given the very low cost per call. But do not expect to notice the effects of a robo call campaign, since it takes roughly 2,000,000 completed calls to produce 1,000 votes.

★★★ *Volunteer phone banks are often effective, but their quality varies, and their capacity to contact large numbers of people is often limited or unpredictable.* The best volunteer phone banks produce one vote per twenty contacts, but half of the volunteer phone banks we studied produced votes at a much lower rate, roughly one voter for every fifty contacts.

★ *Scripts that consist only of a brief reminder seem to produce votes at the lower end of the volunteer phone bank spectrum, yielding approximately one vote per fifty contacts.*

★★ *Live calls conducted by professional phone banks are ineffective, unless callers are coached to deliver messages in a slow and conversational fashion.* Telemarketing firms charge a substantial premium for longer scripts, as using longer scripts increases training costs and reduces the number of calls that can be completed per hour.

★★ *The effectiveness of professional phone banks has little to do with the reasons for voting stressed in the scripts.* Any reasonable script will work or not work, depending on whether it is delivered in an unhurried manner. The three scripts used in the 1998 New Haven and West Haven experiments were equally ineffective. The three scripts used in the 2002 Youth Vote experiment were equally effective.

★★ *Contacting people more than once prior to an election is a waste of resources.* Multiple contacts have no apparent benefits when volunteers make the calls. They seem to accomplish little when the last in a series of calls is a brief, scripted reminder to vote. The sole instance in which repeated calls seem to enhance turnout is when the calls are conducted by well-coached professional callers, who introduce each follow-up call by alluding to past calls and deliver the scripts in an unhurried fashion. Here, however, it is the late timing of the call that matters, not the number of times a person is called.

★★ *Calls are most effective during the last week prior to the election.* Calls made earlier than this do not appear to influence voter turnout.

Cost-Effectiveness

Gauging the cost-effectiveness of alternative phone bank strategies is no simple matter, because the effectiveness of phone banks varies markedly depending on how the callers are trained and supervised. When commercial phone banks deliver uninspired, mechanical messages, they perhaps generate votes at the rate of one per 400 completed calls. At a rate of $0.50 per completed call, that amounts to $200 per additional vote.

On the other hand, top-of-the-line commercial phone banks cost $1.50 per completed call. It is easy to burn a lot of money paying this type of phone bank to make early calls and to call each respondent repeatedly, but a properly targeted campaign can pay off. Suppose this phone bank had contacted voters just once during the last week of the campaign. Assuming that votes were produced at a rate of one per thirty contacts, the cost per vote would be $45 per vote. Obviously, this rate would fall if you were to bargain down the price to, say, $1 per contact. Bear in mind, however, that these figures presuppose a great deal of supervision and training, without which the quality and effectiveness of the calls may well deteriorate.

For phone banks staffed by paid volunteers, votes are produced at a rate of approximately one per thirty-five contacts (contacts here include messages left with housemates). If volunteers are paid at a rate of $16 per hour and make sixteen such contacts per hour, then one additional vote costs $35. Obviously, lower wage rates mean better cost-efficiency, but higher supervision and training costs work in the opposite direction. Most important, the cost of recruiting and maintaining a sufficient number of volunteers to staff a sizable phone bank campaign drives up the cost of a volunteer operation. So, as you reflect on your own circumstances, ask yourself the following questions: How much dependable and committed labor can I muster and at what hourly rate? Do I have easy access to the resources that make a volunteer phone bank run smoothly (for example, phones, supervisory staff)? Finally, what are the opportunity costs of choosing either a commercial or a volunteer phone bank?

The last question deserves special consideration in the light of your campaign's goals. Using a commercial phone bank to propel you to victory may make the celebration a somewhat lonely affair. Those who lament the professionalization of politics point out that the advent of commercial phone banks means that fewer local people participate in campaigns and that the pool of political activists gradually diminishes. If you rely on local activists, you may be able to ask them for labor and political support in the future. Thus the question of how to run a cost-efficient campaign is in part a matter of taking into account future costs and benefits.

Assessment and Conclusions

Although telephone communication is more than a century old, it continues to evolve rapidly. Cellular phones, once the province of science fiction, are now as common as the microwave oven. Yet more than 95 percent of registered voters still live in households with "land line" telephones as well. A large and growing number of residences have caller identification technology, yet fewer than 5 percent of all calls from commercial phone banks are blocked as a result. New rules concerning "do not call lists" designed to prevent telemarketers from making unsolicited calls do not apply to political phone banks, but they may discourage vendors who distribute phone databases for both political and other purposes from gathering these numbers. No one knows how these developments will play out in the future. Phone bank campaigns could become considerably more difficult.

As it stands, phone-based GOTV campaigns are a hit-or-miss affair. Robo phone calls may produce wonderful anecdotes about people coming home from work to find a phone message from their favorite celebrity, but the miniscule effect of these calls on turnout continues to defy scientific detection. Live calls made by the typical telemarketing firm are scarcely more effective. Commercial phone banks, when well coached and carefully supervised, can do an excellent job of producing votes, but their cost-effectiveness depends on the premium charged to deliver a longer, more conversational appeal. In terms of cost per vote, high-quality volunteer efforts have an edge over other types of phone banks—when they take shape as planned. Too often, they fall flat and fail to attract sizable numbers of motivated callers. Falling back on temporary workers means incurring all the hassles of maintaining a phone bank operation with very little payoff in terms of votes.

The ability to tailor a phone bank to serve your purposes has much to do with the resources at your disposal. Can you recruit capable volunteers? Do you have the time and energy to devote to overseeing a volunteer phone bank? If you hire a commercial phone bank, will you be able to work out a deal whereby you help to coach and monitor the callers? Can you obtain a voice recording from a celebrity or some other influential person?

If the answer to one or more of these questions is yes, the issue becomes whether phone calls will prove more cost-effective than other GOTV tactics. The evidence to date suggests that the answer may be no, but that too depends on your circumstances. If it is late in the campaign, phone calls may be the only GOTV technique that is feasible on a large scale. In that case, the question of economic efficiency goes out the window, unless you are trying to save some cash for the next campaign.

Many questions about phone banks remain unanswered. Can volunteer efforts be made more effective, perhaps by assigning people to be in charge of mobilizing their friends and neighbors? Are robo calls incapable of having a big influence on the recipient, or are there ways to give them greater impact, perhaps by "personalizing" them in some fashion? Can the technology of commercial phone banks and the enthusiasm of local volunteers be blended, say by delegating a group of campaign volunteers to work in commercial calling centers? Campaigns may yet discover the optimal mixture of technology and political enthusiasm. For the time being, however, let the buyer beware.

CHAPTER SEVEN

Electronic Mail:
Faster, Cheaper, but Does It Work?

Every new form of communication technology opens new opportunities for mobilizing voters. The explosive growth of the Internet has drawn an increasing number of Americans into the world of electronic mail. According to national surveys, 57 percent of the population used e-mail during 2003, up from 46 percent in 2000.[1] Because both voting and computer use are correlated with income, e-mail usage is especially common among registered voters. Young people are another group that makes frequent use of e-mail. It is estimated that 75 percent of individuals eighteen to twenty-five years of age communicate by e-mail at least once a week.[2]

From the vantage point of campaigns, electronic mail has three attractive properties, at least in principle. First, it enables the sender to reach large numbers of people instantly at very low unit cost. Second, e-mail enables recipients to forward messages easily to their friends, which creates the possibility of extending the influence of a given mailing. Finally, the content of e-mail is very flexible. It is easy to design mailings that direct recipients to websites, which in turn instruct them how to register, where and when to vote, how to find out more about the candidates, and whom to contact in order to become more involved in a campaign.

The downside of e-mail is that recipients are overrun with unsolicited communication, known as spam. Many e-mail servers are equipped with filters that automatically reject or reroute spam. And even when spam wends its way past these filters, there is no guarantee that the recipient will read the message after examining the subject line (the title of the e-mail). Even if the recipient reads your message, there remains the further question of whether this medium actually generates votes. It is one thing to present recipients with options that they can choose immediately from the comfort of their chair, such as visiting a website that tells them where to vote, and another to motivate them to get out of that chair on some future date in order to cast a ballot.

In this chapter, we evaluate the effectiveness of get-out-the-vote appeals conveyed by electronic mail. After describing the nuts and bolts of assembling an e-mail campaign, we examine an e-mail GOTV campaign that involved 346,721 college students in nine states prior to the 2002 elections. Although a single GOTV campaign cannot settle the question of whether e-mail is a cost-effective means of mobilizing voters, the results suggest that caution is in order if you intend to use this tactic.

The Nuts and Bolts of an E-Mail Campaign

Depending on your familiarity with computers, the prospect of sending a mass mailing of e-mail is either daunting or a source of techie excitement. Regardless of whether you distribute the e-mail yourself or rely on a commercial firm, the basic requirements are the same. You will need a mailing list and a message. The challenge is to find the right list and the right message.

Lists

Like phone and direct mail campaigns, e-mail campaigns require a target list. These lists come in three forms. The first is an "opt-in" list of e-mails—addresses supplied by individuals who wish to be contacted by your campaign. Lists of this kind are hard to come by because they require advance work on somebody's part. For example, when registering new voters, you can encourage them to provide their e-mail address so that you can remind them when and where to vote. Some commercial vendors sell opt-in lists, obtained by asking vast numbers of e-mail addressees whether they are willing to receive political communications via e-mail. What counts as opting in varies from vendor to vendor. High quality opt-in lists include only those people who actively consent to receive political e-mail. Low-quality lists contain names of people who did not object when offered the opportunity to receive political spam. This type of opt-in list might be called a "neglected to opt out" list, since many of the people on it simply failed to read or answer their e-mail. The quality of an opt-in list determines its price. High-quality commercial opt-in lists are often quite expensive, somewhere on the order of $0.50 per name. Bear in mind that $0.50 buys one brief live phone call or ten robo calls.

The second type of list is an administrative database maintained by a particular group or organization. For example, colleges typically maintain a directory of their students' e-mail addresses. So do a variety of political organizations. Depending on your connections and the purposes of your campaign, you may be able to purchase these lists. For example, the nonpartisan organization Votes For Students (VFS) was able to purchase the e-mail databases of nineteen colleges, comprising hundreds of thousands of e-mail addresses. The advantage of administrative lists is that they often are linked to mailing addresses, information that allows you to target people in your jurisdiction.

Finally, many commercial vendors supply generic lists of e-mail addresses. How they obtain these addresses is often a mystery. One common technique is to create a program that searches through millions of web pages, harvesting all of the e-mail addresses listed therein. On the one hand, these lists tend to be dirt cheap ($50 will buy millions of addresses). But it is anybody's guess as to whether they contain any registered voters in your jurisdiction. Unless you are especially interested in getting the word out to Internet users in faraway places, you should avoid generic lists.

Messages

An e-mail message should be thought of as three distinct components. The first is the subject line. This line frequently determines whether your message makes it past spam filters designed to prevent mass mailings (such as yours). The more personal the message, the less likely it is to be stopped by filters or shunted to a bulk mail box. There are, of course, all sorts of sleazy tricks to get past these filters, such as using the subject line "MESSAGE RETURNED, NAMESERVER ERROR." Do not resort to these tactics. It is hard to imagine that voters who open an e-mail with this misleading subject line will be receptive to the GOTV message that awaits them. Take the high road and formulate a short phrase that might plausibly encourage recipients to vote in the upcoming election. For example, "Need help finding your polling place in today's election?" or "Lincoln County Elections today: Polls open from 6 a.m. to 8 p.m." This has the added effect of getting the message across even to those who do not open your e-mail.

The second component of an e-mail is the text. How the text looks to readers will depend on the mail browser they are using. Some may read the text as though it were printed by an old-fashioned typewriter; others may be able to appreciate your choice of font and type size. Before sending a message, do a trial run with a few types of mail browsers to see how it will come across. One style of e-mail is to present people with a few simple messages, with web links to follow if they seek additional information. Another is to hit people with a wall of words, as though they are delving into a newspaper story. The former has the advantage of being accessible to most voters, although the latter seems popular in universities, where authoritative-sounding e-mails are sometimes forwarded to friends.

The final aspect of e-mail is graphics. Primitive e-mail readers will not display them, and neither will newer ones that are designed to filter unsolicited and perhaps distasteful images. But most e-mail users see graphics when they open up an e-mail. One advantage of sending graphics is that they make the message more vivid and memorable.

Another advantage of sending e-mail to HTML-compatible e-mail browsers is that your e-mail server is alerted when the message is loaded, enabling you to count the number of messages that have been opened. In one of the experiments described next, this information was crucial: without it, we would not have been able to distinguish an e-mail campaign that failed because no one read the messages from an e-mail campaign that failed because the messages, when read, failed to motivate people to vote.

Experimental Evidence Concerning E-Mail

Evaluating the effectiveness of an e-mail campaign is no mean feat. It is easy to send e-mail, but hard to link e-mail addresses to individual voters. This problem bedeviled the first experimental study of e-mail, conducted during the 2000 campaign by John Phillips of Yale University.[3] His approach was to conduct a postelection survey, by e-mail, of 6,000 young registered voters whose names had been placed into treatment and control groups. The problem with this strategy is that people who received the e-mail encouragement to vote, and did so, might be especially inclined to respond to the survey. In addition, this approach relies on self-reports about voter turnout. The fact that this study found a series of three e-mails to have negligible mobilization effects is suggestive but not reliable.

Fortunately, a golden opportunity for an evaluation of GOTV e-mail presented itself in the form of the Votes for Students campaign in 2002. Votes For Students, as the name suggests, is a nonpartisan organization designed to encourage voter participation by college students. Led by an imaginative and energetic group of University of Minnesota undergraduates, Votes For Students collaborated with colleges to assemble an enormous database of student e-mail addresses.

VFS programmers created a computer platform capable of sending large quantities of e-mail and of monitoring the rate at which these messages were opened. In order to allow for the possibility that students might forward the VFS e-mail to friends, these experimental e-mails were sent out in varying "density" to each campus. Some campuses received a high density of e-mail—half or more of the students received VFS messages. On other campuses less than one-quarter of the students received VFS messages. If students in the treatment group were infecting students in the control group, the low-density schools should show bigger treatment effects than the high-density schools.

The content and frequency of the e-mail varied considerably from school to school, as illustrated in box 7-1. Students attending the University of Minnesota were treated to a dose of school spirit, inasmuch as the six e-mails encouraging voter participation typically ended with the cheer "Go Gophers!" Other schools received fewer e-mail messages because Votes For Students obtained their e-mail databases later than expected. In most cases, students received four e-mails. An early October e-mail conveyed information about how to register to vote. A late October message provided information about how to obtain an absentee ballot. A few days before the election, students were reminded of the importance of voting. A final reminder was sent on election day.

As expected, many of the VFS e-mails went unopened. Combining all of the sites, 26 percent of the recipients opened at least one of the VFS e-mails. (This number is probably an underestimate, because Votes For Students could not tell whether recipients using browsers that do not load HTML images opened their e-mail.) Still, Votes For Students enjoyed remarkable "click-through" rates in some cases. At Georgia Tech, 48 percent of the students opened a VFS e-mail; at University of Wisconsin-Madison, the rate was 62 percent. At a minimum, students were exposed to a series of e-mail subject lines that called attention to voter registration deadlines and the impending election.

The massive size of the experiment enabled us to pinpoint the effect of e-mail with a high degree of precision. After the election was over, these colleges furnished home addresses, campus addresses, or both for

---

Box 7-1. Text of the Six E-Mail Messages Sent to University of Minnesota Students

1. Subject line: Deadline Oct. 15, Register to Vote Online Today.
As college students we have made excuses for too long about why we don't vote. We need to stop ignoring our duty and just do it. Votes For Students is a nonpartisan organization that gives you all the voting tools needed to stop making excuses. By clicking on the link below, you can get a voter registration form, access an absentee ballot online, and more. As college students, let's stop neglecting democracy. VOTE. Oh, and enjoy homecoming. GO GOPHERS!

2. Subject line: Online Voter Registration: Deadline Tuesday
Fellow U of M students
For the past two years we have seen huge tuition increases because not enough students vote. We as students need to change that. It is now possible by clicking on the link below to download a voter registration form and get access to an absentee ballot online. Take advantage of how easy it is to vote these days and do your part to stop the tuition increases. VOTE. Oh, and enjoy homecoming. GO GOPHERS!

3a. Subject line: Request an Absentee Ballot Online Today
College students are some of the busiest people around. We know because we are students like you. To make your life easier we have taken away all the hassles of voting this fall. By clicking on the link below, you can get voter registration forms, access an absentee ballot online, and more. Take advantage of how quick and easy voting is this fall. Oh, and enjoy homecoming. GO GOPHERS.

3b. Subject Line: Reminder: Get your Absentee Ballot Today
As we saw in Florida, one vote can make a difference, your vote. Votes For

---

the students in the treatment and control groups. We then matched these names and addresses to the voter rolls in order to see which students registered or voted. Undoubtedly, some of these addresses were out of date, but our capacity to match names accurately was identical for treatment and control groups, and the results remained unchanged when we increased the stringency of the matching criteria.

Students is a student-run, nonpartisan organization working to give you everything you need to make your vote count. By clicking on the link below, you can get a voter registration form, access absentee ballots online, and more. Register, VOTE, make a difference. Oh, and enjoy homecoming. GO GOPHERS!

4. Subject line: Express your opinion on politics
Votes For Students would like to hear your opinion. Tell us what you think of politics and you will be eligible to win cash prizes of up to $500. By answering the question below as well as a short series of questions that will follow, you can help us learn about the student voice. Tell us your opinion and, more importantly, VOTE.

5. Subject line: Vote Tuesday Nov. 5
Voting in Minnesota is as simple as voting gets. With same-day voter registration, Minnesota citizens can vote even if they missed earlier registration deadlines. All you need to do is take a picture ID (student ID is acceptable) and proof of your address. Do your part. VOTE Tuesday, November 5.

6. Subject line: Vote Today: Vote Tuesday Nov. 5
A single vote can make a difference. Your vote. As we have seen in recent elections, one vote has the power to decide the future direction of our country. Your vote will impact the way our government addresses terrorism, education, the economy, and every other aspect of your life. And in Minnesota every citizen over eighteen can go to the polls and make a difference. All you need to do is take a picture ID (student ID is acceptable) and proof of your address. Do your part. VOTE Today.

We looked for evidence that students in the treatment group registered to vote and voted at higher rates than students in the control group. We were surprised that neither proved to be the case. Although "click-through" data showed that Votes For Students directed more than 10,000 people to a website that enabled them to register to vote online, the treatment group was no more likely to be registered to vote than the control group. Either the people directed to online registration failed to register, or they would have registered anyway, without the e-mail stimulus. By the same token, the turnout rates for the treatment group were no higher than for the control group. For example, the registration rate among the 34,585 University of Minnesota students in the treatment group was 50.7 percent. The registration rate among the 1,820 students in the control group was also 50.7 percent. The voter turnout rate in the treatment group was 39.7 percent, compared with 39.3 percent in the control group. But this small and statistically unreliable positive effect was offset by results from other sites, some of which showed small negative effects. Overall, the estimated effect was very slightly negative.

In order to double-check these results, we focused special attention on four schools in California, Georgia, and Michigan. These schools supplied home addresses for each of the students, so it was clear which students potentially were registered out-of-state. In order to guard against the possibility that Votes For Students encouraged people in the treatment group to register out-of-state (in which case we would not find them on the state's voter rolls and would infer mistakenly that they had not voted), we eliminated all students from both treatment and control groups who had an out-of-state home address. The results remained unchanged. Among in-state students, VFS e-mails increased neither registration nor turnout rates.

This pattern of null results held regardless of whether the state had a traditional voting system (California, Georgia, Maryland), a prevoting period (Colorado), or same-day voter registration (Minnesota, Wisconsin). None of the sixteen sites showed positive mobilization effects that were greater than would be expected by chance.

Lessons Learned

The lessons emerging from these studies are rated according to the system detailed in chapter 2: three stars are for findings that have received solid confirmation from several experiments, two stars are for more equivocal findings based on one or two experiments, and one star is for findings that are suggestive but not conclusive.

★★ *Nonpartisan e-mail designed to encourage voter participation has negligible effects on voter registration.* Although thousands of recipients of these e-mails followed links to sites where they could register online, registration rates for the treatment and control groups were almost identical. Absent this e-mail campaign, the people who registered online would have registered anyway.

★★ *E-mail appears to have negligible effects on voter turnout.* Despite the large samples used in this study, we found no evidence that e-mail raised turnout.

Assessment and Conclusion

Given the current state of the evidence, the cost assessment of electronic mail is rather dismal. Setting up a target database and hiring technical staff to design and distribute e-mail involves substantial start-up costs. Although the VFS program was run by a team of capable volunteers, the database alone cost approximately $15,000. The marginal cost of sending each e-mail was minimal, but unfortunately, the effects on registration and turnout were minimal as well.

Although the overall picture is one of small effects, there remains a glimmer of hope for e-mail. Given the tiny marginal costs of sending e-mail, it does not require much of an effect for e-mail to be a cost-effective means of mobilizing voters. The challenge for e-mail campaigns, then, is to experiment with a variety of approaches, in search of an appeal that works reliably. Disappointing as the VFS results are, they are hardly proof that e-mail campaigns are doomed to fail. Could the way forward be more personalized e-mail, perhaps propagated by friends encouraging each other to vote?

CHAPTER EIGHT

Frontiers of Get-Out-the-Vote Research

The dozens of experiments summarized in this book provide a useful benchmark for anyone seeking to launch or evaluate a voter mobilization campaign. When we began our experimental research in 1998, we were struck by the fact that even people running very expensive campaigns were operating on little more than their own intuition about what worked. The academic literature in existence at that time was little help. Experimental studies were rare, and the ones that found their way into print reported what we now know to be outlandish findings. One study, based on interviews with fewer than 100 college students, purported to show that calling people up on election eve and asking them whether they intended to vote increased their probability of doing so by more than 20 percentage points.[1] Bear in mind that the callers did not implore people to vote; they merely inquired about plans to vote yet generated a massive "self-prophecy effect." Another study, also based on a few dozen voters, purported to show that partisan mail increased turnout 19 percentage points.[2]

With a mix of optimism and skepticism, we have spent the last few years replicating the studies that claimed to have discovered giant effects. After all, if these effects were truly as the authors described them, low voter turnout could be cured with a nationwide survey or a massive direct mail campaign. Alas, we and other researchers have found that a single mailing has a modest effect on turnout, raising it less than half of a percentage point. Asking people whether they intended to vote proved to be a nonstarter as well. An experiment with our Yale collaborators Jennifer Smith and Anton Orlich debunked the notion of a "self-prophecy effect."[3]

More than 1,000 Connecticut voters were queried about their intentions to vote, but turnout remained unchanged. Similarly, another Yale researcher, Christopher Mann, found that preelection phone interviews by *Washington Post* pollsters had no effect on turnout.[4] The list of registered voters who were slated for calls had the same voting rate as a randomly selected control group that was left alone. Merely asking people about their views of the candidates or their intentions to vote did not increase their chances of voting.

With the benefit of hindsight, these findings make perfect sense. Robo calls imploring people to vote have little effect. The same goes for live calls from most commercial phone banks. If urging people to vote has little impact, it would be amazing if one could raise turnout rates just by asking people whether they planned to vote. As for direct mail, we now know that one cannot detect its small effects unless one studies thousands of voters. A study of a few dozen people—or even a few hundred people—may announce the discovery of huge effects simply due to chance. Looking back, it seems clear that these sensational findings can be attributed to something called "publication bias." Academic journals are averse to publishing statistically insignificant findings, which means that smaller studies must report larger results if they are to find their way into print. As a result, the experimental studies that find their way into print tend to give a misleading picture of what works.[5]

And those are just the experimental studies. If we expand the discussion of unreliable evidence to include nonexperimental research—such as focus groups, surveys, and case histories that do not involve control groups—the litany of unsupported claims becomes nearly boundless. These claims are not necessarily false, just untrustworthy. One wonders whether researchers are doing anything more than expressing their intuitions in scientific parlance.

Once the red herrings have been cleared from the path, the experimental results form an intelligible pattern. We begin by summarizing what *does not* work.

✔ Mobilizing voters is not merely a matter of reminding them that election day is near. Prerecorded messages reminding people to vote do little, if anything, to raise turnout, even when the prerecorded voices are those of well-known and credible people. E-mail reminders to register and vote appear to be ineffective as well.

✔ Mobilizing voters is not simply a matter of engaging their attention. Live calls from commercial phone banks typically have weak effects. Voters listen to the brief script and overwhelmingly reply yes when asked whether they plan to vote. Yet one experiment after another shows that we know from voter turnout records that people in the treatment group are scarcely more likely to vote than those in the control group.

✔ Mobilizing voters is not just a matter of supplying them with information about the candidates. Canvassing campaigns that distribute voter guides are not noticeably more successful than canvassing campaigns that do not do so.

Having ruled out several explanations, we now offer some hypotheses that seem to be suggested by the experimental results.

✔ To mobilize voters, you must make them feel wanted at the polls. Mobilizing voters is rather like inviting them to a social occasion. Personal invitations convey the most warmth and work best. Next best are phone calls in which the caller converses with the respondent, as opposed to reading a canned script. Less effective but still somewhat helpful are mailed invitations.

✔ Building on voters' preexisting level of motivation to vote is also important. Frequent voters, by definition, have demonstrated their willingness to participate in the electoral process. In low-turnout elections, they are especially receptive to get-out-the-vote appeals, particularly when contacted face-to-face.

If belongingness and motivation play pivotal roles, it follows that more intensive treatments along these lines should have even bigger effects. This expectation was borne out by an interesting series of experiments aimed at high school seniors. Working with five schools in Connecticut during the 2002–03 academic year, Yale researchers Elizabeth Addonizio, David Ogle, and Beth Weinberger randomly divided each senior class in half.[6] Students selected for the treatment group were placed into small groups of roughly a dozen students. Each of these groups was given a pep talk about the importance of voting in the upcoming election, an opportunity to register to vote, and a chance to cast a mock ballot using the actual voting machines that were to be used in their jurisdiction. Notice that this intervention was a far cry from merely distributing pamphlets explaining the voting process. The hour-long session enabled students to ask questions and walk though the voting process, so as to overcome any anxieties they might have about casting their first vote.

High school voting seminars proved to be enormously effective. Turnout in the control group was just 11 percent, compared with 25 percent among those assigned to the treatment group—a statistically significant difference. And if we take into account the fact that only two-thirds of those who were assigned to the treatment group actually showed up for the session (some students mysteriously disappeared en route to the GOTV classroom), attendance at the voter education session increased voter turnout 20 percentage points. That is, for every five students who attended the sessions, one additional voter was produced.

The same logic suggests that the effects of some of the GOTV tactics we describe here could be enhanced if they were made more intensive. For example, anonymous e-mail seems to do little to increase voter turnout, but what about e-mail from personal friends? Canvassing by campaign workers typically increases turnout, but would the effects be larger if the canvasser were a candidate or a neighbor? We strongly suspect that enhancing the personal feel of these GOTV tactics would increase their impact, but we do not yet have direct evidence. Looking at the effects of "super-treatments" represents an important new frontier in this line of research.

Summarizing the Cost-Effectiveness of GOTV Tactics

Table 8-1 summarizes our assessment of the bottom line. What does it cost to make a voter out of someone who would otherwise abstain? Each of the GOTV tactics is characterized in terms of costs and benefits. As you examine this table, remember that the attractiveness of any GOTV tactic depends on the resources available to your campaign and the constraints within which it operates. If your campaign is long on enthusiastic volunteers but short on money, you might consider leafleting, canvassing, or conducting a volunteer phone bank. If your campaign has money but lacks volunteers, you might invest your money in carefully supervised commercial phone banks or perhaps direct mail.

One of the most important lessons to draw from table 8-1 is that conventional GOTV campaigns seldom work miracles. Canvassing 100 registered voters at their doorstep will not generate 100 votes. A more realistic estimate is seven additional votes. Similarly, sending a piece of direct mail to 10,000 partisan supporters will not bring 10,000 people to the polls. The number of additional voters you should realistically expect from this type of direct mail campaign is fifty-six.

Table 8-1. Cost-Effectiveness of Get-Out-the-Vote Tactics[a]

GOTV effort	Start-up costs	Supervising costs	Effectiveness per contact[b]	Dollar cost per vote
Door-to-door[c]	Labor intensive: amassing walkers and creating walk lists	Substantial ongoing training and supervision	One vote per 14 contacts (excludes spillover)	At $16 an hour and 12 contacts an hour, one vote costs $19, plus overhead
Leafleting[c]	Labor intensive: recruiting walkers, creating walk lists, designing and printing leaflets, providing personalized polling locations	Monitoring walkers		
Partisan			One vote per 66 registered voters "contacted"	At $10 an hour and 45 leaflets an hour, $0.10 per leaflet, one vote costs $14 (?), plus overhead
Nonpartisan			One vote per 200 voters "contacted"	At $10 an hour, 45 leaflets an hour, and $0.10 per leaflet, one vote costs $43 (?), plus overhead
Direct mail[c]	Resource intensive: designing, printing, and mailing	Intensive during start-up, then Postal Service takes over		
Partisan base			One vote per 177 recipients	At $0.50 per piece, one vote costs $59
Other partisan			One vote per 600 recipients	$200 per vote
Nonpartisan			One vote per 200 recipients	$67 per vote
Phone				
Volunteer, partisan or nonpartisan	Labor intensive: amassing enthusiastic callers and securing phone bank	Ongoing training and supervision	One vote per 35 contacts	At $16 an hour and 16 contacts per hour, one vote costs $35
Commercial live calls, no special coaching	Resource intensive: contract out to phone bank	Ongoing or sporadic monitoring	One vote per 400 completed calls	At a rate of $0.50 per completed call, one vote costs $200
Commercial live calls, special coaching, long scripts	Same as above	Extensive monitoring	One vote per 30 completed calls	At $1.50 per completed call, one vote costs $45
Robo calls	Same as above	None	No detectable effect	
E-mail	Moderately labor intensive: amass e-mail lists, write message(s)	Most of the work is in the start-up	No detectable effect	

a. Costs may vary due to local circumstances and market conditions.

b. "Contact" is defined as follows: for door-to-door, talking to target or other voters living at the same address; for phone calls, talking or leaving a message; for mail, mail sent; for leaflets, leaflet dropped at door.

c. Assumes that the average household has 1.5 voters.

We are not saying that GOTV work is fruitless. Our point is rather that an ambitious GOTV campaign requires a serious investment in both quality and quantity. In order to generate 1,000 votes, your door-to-door canvassing effort may need to visit 30,000 addresses, making contact with 14,000 registered voters. Or you could send out 130,000 mailers, or hire a high-quality commercial phone bank to call 60,000 households, reading a lengthy script to 30,000 registered voters who are willing to listen. Each of these approaches relies on the *scale* of a well-crafted GOTV operation to generate appreciable numbers of additional votes.

Another approach is to place even greater emphasis on the quality of GOTV work. We have alluded to the possibility of super-treatments that may produce much bigger mobilization effects than the treatments we analyze in other chapters. A call or visit by a charismatic candidate, as opposed to a volunteer canvasser, might well produce larger effects. If you are contemplating a campaign that emphasizes quality, keep things in perspective. Even if your super-treatments are twice as effective as the most effective door-to-door canvassing campaign, you will still need to contact 7,000 registered voters to produce 1,000 votes. And contacting 7,000 registered voters means visiting roughly 15,000 households. To sway election outcomes involving large numbers of voters, high-quality campaigns must also be high-quantity campaigns.

Further Thoughts on Cost-Effectiveness: Mobilizing Voters over the Long Haul

Voter turnout campaigns tend to focus on the here and now. They work to generate votes during the waning days of the campaign, and when the polls close, the campaign closes shop as well. Apart from influencing the outcome of an election, what lasting effects do GOTV campaigns have?

One of the most interesting findings to emerge from GOTV research is that voter mobilization campaigns have enduring effects. The New Haven residents who were randomly assigned to receive direct mail or face-to-face canvassing in 1998 were more likely to vote in both the 1998 November election and in the mayoral election held in November 1999.[7] This study has since been replicated with nine other canvassing populations.[8] Taken together, these studies show that for every 100 voters mobilized in a given election, an additional thirty-three will participate in the following election. If we assume a geometrically declining rate over time, 100 additional votes in this year's election will produce a total of forty-eight additional votes in all subsequent elections.

The long-term impact of voter mobilization has profound implications. First, it suggests that voting is a habit-forming activity. Someone who votes in this election is more likely to vote in the next election. Someone who skips an election is less likely to vote in the future. Perhaps America's low turnout rates reflect the fact that we have the most frequent elections on earth. One might liken sleepy municipal elections to gateway drugs; by enticing so many people to abstain from voting, they weaken voting habits.

Second, this finding casts a different light on the usual way of evaluating the costs and benefits of a GOTV campaign. The typical approach is to think only in terms of votes produced in the current election. A more realistic calculation would take into account the future effects of this year's voter mobilization drive. If your campaign generates 1,000 additional votes at a cost of $40,000, this price amounts to $40 per vote for the current election. But if we also include the 330 votes in the next election, the price falls to $40,000/1,330 = $30 per vote. This added efficiency is an important consideration for political parties and other organizations that have a long-term interest in producing votes, especially if the alternative is to spend money on persuasive messages that may have no long-term impact once the current slate of candidates has moved on.

Synergy?

One common refrain among those who design campaigns is the importance of "touching" voters with all sorts of different forms of campaign communication. Touch them first with a mailer, then with a phone call, then with another mailer, and so forth. When thinking about the cost-effectiveness of this approach, it is important to be clear about exactly what is being claimed. A GOTV campaign consisting of a mailer and a phone call probably will produce more votes than a campaign consisting of just a phone call or just a mailer. The notion that "more is better" is not really at issue here. When consultants speak of an "integrated" campaign in which the whole is greater than the sum of the parts, they are suggesting that those who receive mail are *especially* responsive to the ensuing phone call (or vice versa). Suppose that mail increases turnout 1 percent and phone contact increases it 2 percent. The claim is that mail and phone together increase turnout more than 3 percent.

Not one of the experiments involving multiple treatments lends support to this claim. In the 1998 New Haven study, mail did not increase the effectiveness of phone calls or door-to-door canvassing. In the 2000

NAACP National Voter Fund study, those who received mail were as (weakly) influenced by phone calls as those who received no mail. The 2002 NALEO experiment failed to support the hypothesis that robo calls enhance the effectiveness of direct mail or vice versa. Neither direct mail nor robo calls amplified the effects of live calls. Special combinations of GOTV appeals do not appear to deliver a bonus of votes.

Perhaps the reason for the lack of synergy has to do with the mechanisms by which GOTV campaigns work. Getting a piece of direct mail rarely creates a personal sense of belonging, so the subsequent phone call does not build on a growing predisposition to vote. Conversely, for those who have received a phone call, the ensuing mailer does not have special resonance. Although it is possible to imagine a situation in which one GOTV tactic amplifies the effect of another, we have not seen evidence of these interaction effects. That explains why this book is organized into chapters that look at GOTV tactics one at a time rather than in special combinations.

Filling in the Blanks: What Is the Role of the Mass Media?

One important gap in our knowledge concerns the influence of the mass media. Whether we are talking about television, radio, billboards, or newspaper ads, the effects of both paid advertising and public service announcements remain a mystery. The depth of ignorance on this subject is surprising given the amount of money at stake. Yet, so far as we know, not a single randomized experiment on political media has been conducted in the real world.[9]

Instead, those who study media effects have been content to conduct surveys and laboratory experiments. A typical survey examines the correlation between political opinions and the advertisements shown in various media markets. The problem with this approach is that the ads are not randomly assigned to different media markets. If the people who watch GOP ads on television are unusually prone to vote Republican, does that mean that ads shape opinions or that the ads happen to be viewed by Republican audiences? In response to this fundamental complaint, survey analysts generate a welter of statistics designed to make ad viewers as comparable as possible to non-viewers, but a half-century of this line of research has brought us no closer to the answer.

During the last two decades, researchers have attempted to grapple with the problem of uncertain causation by conducting laboratory experiments. Here, subjects are randomly assigned to view television shows with varying advertising content. For example, one group of people might be shown a news broadcast that contains a set of ads extolling the virtues of one of the candidates, while another group might be shown the same show, but with the same candidate's harshly worded attack ads.

Experiments of this kind suffer from several drawbacks. One limitation is that most studies relate media exposure to the *intention* to vote rather than to actual voting. In other words, shortly after watching the shows, subjects in the experiment fill out a questionnaire asking whether they intend to vote. That raises the question of whether these intentions persist. Using a group of survey respondents who were shown ads via Web-TV, our Yale colleague John Lapinski and his co-author Joshua Clinton demonstrated that when researchers follow up with subjects after the election and ask whether they voted, the experimental treatment effects disappear.[10] Another drawback of laboratory studies is that they examine behavior in a contrived setting. The ordinary person is seldom paid to watch television. The ordinary person is seldom invited to watch television for research purposes. The ordinary person has access to a remote control with which to change channels. How results obtained in the lab translate into voter turnout in the outside world therefore remains unclear.

As we write, our research team is embarking on a new line of field experiments designed to study the effects of the mass media. Media markets will be randomly assigned to treatment and control groups, and voter turnout within these geographic areas will be compared. Our findings will be reported in subsequent editions of this book, but for now we venture the following hypothesis: television and radio messages that urge voter participation or simply advocate support for a candidate have little influence on voter turnout. Our reasoning—which may well prove incorrect—is that the messages are conveyed in an impersonal manner and therefore do little to overcome the psychological barriers to voting.

Conducting Your Own Experiment

The experiments described in this book have only begun to scratch the surface of all that can be learned about making GOTV campaigns more efficient. While reading this book, you may have thought of some experiments of your own. You may be running for office, wondering how you can use the lessons learned from your upcoming campaign to improve the efficiency of subsequent campaigns. Or perhaps you remain unpersuaded by the experimental results presented in this book and want to see for yourself whether they hold up.

With a bit of forethought, you should be able to put a meaningful experiment into place. You do not need an advanced degree in social science, but it is important to plan carefully so as to guard against the problems that sometimes confront this type of research. Here is a brief overview of how experiments are designed, conducted, and analyzed.

Spell out your hypothesis. Although it sounds like a class assignment, a useful first step in any experimental project is to write, in a single sentence, the claim that you will be testing. This will force you to clarify what the treatment is and who the subjects are. For example, "Among voters with Latino surnames, Spanish-language mailers increase turnout more than English-language mailers," or "Candidates are better able to mobilize voters through door-to-door canvassing than are the activists who work for candidates," or "Election day rides increase voter turnout among those who live more than a mile from their polling place."

Define your target list. Create a list of voters who will be targeted for the GOTV intervention you are evaluating. Depending on how your campaign is organized, the lists of targets may be individual people or places (such as voting precincts). For example, your list may consist of Latino voters in Denver County.

Determine how many people (or places) you wish to assign to the treatment and control categories. The larger the numbers in each category, the more precise your results will be. However, do not assign more people to the treatment group than you have the resources to treat. Apportion your experimental groups so that your contact rate in the treatment group will be as high as possible. Box 8-1 offers some sense of how precise your estimates will be under different allocation schemes.

Divide the list into treatment and control groups. Creating random treatment and control groups is easy to do with a spreadsheet program such as Microsoft Excel. Box 8-2 walks you through the steps of randomly sorting and subdividing your target list.

Random sorting is useful even if you are apprehensive about excluding a control group. Suppose you are conducting a phone canvass. Sort your phone list so that it is in random order. Call through the randomly sorted list, starting from the top and working your way down. When your campaign is over, any names that you did not attempt to call represent your control group. The names that you did attempt to call represent the treatment group.[11] Nothing about the campaign's execution has changed, but now it becomes amenable to rigorous evaluation in the

---

Box 8-1. Calculating the Precision of an Experiment

With calculator in hand, you can easily anticipate the precision of an experiment. Let C represent the contact rate (the proportion of people in the treatment group that you actually contacted). A typical contact rate for a phone experiment is 0.5, for example. Let N represent the number of people on your list. Let N_T stand for the number of people in your treatment group and N_C, the number of people in your control group. The margin of error in your study is plus or minus the square root of N divided by the square root of $(C^2 N_T N_C)$. So, if your contact rate is 0.5, 9,000 people are in the treatment group, and 1,000 people are in the control group, then your margin of error is 0.067, or 6.7 percentage points. In other words, if you add and subtract 6.7 percentage points from whatever result you obtain, you will have a 95 percent chance of bracketing the true effect of your intervention. If that margin of error seems uncomfortably large, increase the sample size, make the control group and treatment group closer in size, or improve the contact rate.

---

event that you fail to attempt all of the names on your target list. This approach is ideal for evaluating campaigns whose goals outstrip their resources.

Check the randomization. Random assignment should, in principle, create treatment and control groups that have similar background characteristics. To make sure that you have conducted the randomization properly, check to see that the treatment and control groups have approximately the same rate of voter turnout in some recent election (before your intervention). If this information is not available, check to see that the average age in the treatment group is approximately the same as the average age in the control group. If the treatment and control groups differ appreciably, you may have made a computer error. Redo your randomization.

Administer the treatment to the treatment group only. Be vigilant about adhering to the treatment and control assignments. Do not contact anyone on the control list! The easiest way to keep the experiment from going awry is to release only the treatment names to the phone bank or direct mail vendor. Send leafleteers and door-to-door canvassers out with names of people in the treatment group (only) and remind them not to knock blindly on every door.

Box 8-2. Random Assignment

Random assignment to treatment and control groups is easily accomplished with a spreadsheet program such as Microsoft Excel. First, open the spreadsheet containing the list of voters. Second, place your cursor on an empty cell in the spreadsheet and click the equal sign in order to call up the equation editor. Enter the formula RAND() and hit enter. A random number between 0 and 1 should appear in the cell. Second, copy and paste this random number into a column beside the columns in your data set. Now every row in your data set should contain a random number. Fourth, highlight all of the columns in your data set and click DATA > SORT. A box should appear asking you to indicate which column(s) to sort by. Choose the column that corresponds to the column of random numbers just generated. Click OK. Fifth, having sorted the data in random order, add a new column to your data set. This new column will indicate whether each person is assigned to the treatment group. If you want 500 people in your treatment group, put the number 1 into the first 500 rows and the number 0 into the remaining rows.

Maintain records of who was contacted, even if that person is someone in the control group who was contacted by mistake. You will need this information in order to calculate the effect of actually receiving your intervention.

Once you have successfully carried out this protocol, you can take a breather until voting data become available following the election. This can take several weeks or months. You will probably have to keep checking in with registrars or data vendors. While you wait, and before you forget the details, write up the description of the experiment and how it was conducted.

When voter turnout data become available, calculate the turnout rates of the people in the treatment and control groups. You can do this by hand or by computer using the subjects' names and voter identification numbers.

Analyze the experimental results. The difference in turnout between the *original* treatment and control groups—ignoring for the moment whether persons in the treatment group were actually treated—tells you quite a lot. If the turnout rate in the assigned treatment group is higher,

Box 8-3. Simplified Web Software
for Analyzing Experimental Data

For the convenience of first-time experimenters, we have created a website (research.yale.edu/vote) that reads in experimental results and generates a statistical analysis. You supply six numbers: the number of people that you (1) assigned to the treatment group, (2) assigned to the control group, (3) successfully treated in the treatment group, (4) inadvertently treated in the control group, (5) found to have voted in the treatment group, and (6) found to have voted in the control group.

To see how the program works, suppose you wish to analyze results from Melissa Michelson's door-to-door canvassing experiment in Dos Palos, California. Prior to the 2001 election, she assigned 466 people with Latino surnames to the treatment group and 298 Latinos to the control group. Of the people in the treatment group, 342 were successfully contacted. No one in the control group was contacted. In the treatment group, eighty-six people voted, whereas forty-one people voted in the control group. The six inputs are, therefore, 466, 298, 342, 0, 86, 41.

After entering these numbers in the appropriate boxes, click the "Submit" button. You will see output that summarizes the research findings and estimates the size and precision of the treatment effects. Check the statistical summary that appears in the middle of the page in order to ensure that you have entered the data correctly. The computer will summarize the voting rates and contact rates based on the numbers you provided. Next, examine the "intent-to-treat" estimate. This number is calculated by subtracting the voting rate in the control group from the voting rate in the group assigned to the treatment. In this example, the intent-to-treat estimate is 4.7, suggesting that assignment to the treatment group raised turnout

your intervention succeeded in raising turnout. This difference is known as the intent-to-treat effect, because it does not take notice of the possibility that only some of the assigned treatment group was actually treated.

Next calculate the contact rate. Divide the number contacted in the treatment group by the number of people assigned to the treatment group. If your contact rate is less than 100 percent, divide the intent-to-treat effect by the contact rate. This number indicates the effect of the treatment on those who were actually treated. Consider this example: Your control group votes at a rate of 42 percent. Your treatment group

4.7 percentage points. Beneath this figure is the standard error of the esti-mated intent-to-treat effect. The larger this number, the more uncertainty surrounds the intent-to-treat estimate. The "treatment effect" is estimated by dividing the intent-to-treat estimate (4.7) by the contact rate (0.73), which produces the number 6.4. Those who were actually treated became 6.4 per-centage points more likely to vote. The uncertainty of this estimate is meas-ured by its standard error, 3.7.

Finally, the statistical software makes three useful calculations. The first is the 95 percent confidence interval, which spans from –0.8 to 13.6. The true treatment effect has a 95 percent probability of lying within this range. The second calculation is the one-tailed significance of the estimated treat-ment effect. When conducting GOTV experiments, it is conventional to expect turnout to rise as a result of the treatment. The so-called "null hypothesis" is that the treatment failed to increase turnout. The one-tailed significance level states the probability of obtaining an estimate as large as the estimated treatment effect (in this case 6.4) by chance. When this prob-ability is below 0.05, as is the case here, the estimate is said to be "statisti-cally significant." Naturally, if the experiment were repeated, the results might come out differently. The "power" of an experiment describes the probability that it will produce a statistically significant estimate given the observed treatment effect. In this case, Michelson's experiment has a 54 percent probability of rejecting the null hypothesis given that the treatment effect is 6.4. The power of an experiment can be improved by raising the contact rate or increasing the number of observations.

votes at a rate of 47 percent. Your contact rate is 50 percent. So the effect of the treatment on the treated is $(47 - 42)/0.5 = 10$ percentage points.

Perform a statistical analysis. A bit of statistical analysis can indicate how likely it is that the difference you are seeing might have been pro-duced by chance. Why worry about chance? Sometimes just by luck of the draw you may underestimate or overestimate the effectiveness of the treatment. We have developed some (free) web tools to walk you through this process as painlessly as possible and to give you some point-ers about how to interpret the numbers (see box 8-3).

Crafting an experiment requires careful planning and supervision, yet experience has shown that novices can do it. For years we have taught an undergraduate class that requires students to conduct a full-fledged randomized study. We also teach a summer workshop on experiments, attended by faculty, students, and nonacademics. Several students from both of these seminars have gone on to conduct clever and well-executed voter mobilization studies. One student got a team of friends together to make GOTV calls on behalf of a Democratic candidate for governor; another student designed and distributed nonpartisan direct mail; another organized a large-scale precinct walking campaign.

Such experimental studies require a fair amount of effort, but the biggest hurdle in conducting a successful experiment is conceptual. To design and execute a randomized experiment, you must first understand why a randomly assigned control group is essential. At every stage in the process of executing an experiment, people will whine about your insistence on a control group. They will propose instead that you simply consider the people they fail to contact as the control group, oblivious to the fact that this approach would ruin the study. You will have to convince them that a randomly assigned control group is indispensable.

To do so, the following example may be helpful. In the process of developing a vaccine to eliminate polio, scientists needed to assess whether the vaccine worked and to determine its side effects.[12] They randomly assigned hundreds of thousands of children to receive one of two types of shots: approximately 200,000 children received the real vaccine, and another 200,000 received an identical-looking placebo. Roughly fifty children who received the vaccine contracted polio, as opposed to 150 who received the placebo. Without a high-quality experiment, scientists would not have known two key facts about this vaccine: it helped to reduce the incidence of polio, but it was far from perfect. On the basis of this experiment, the vaccine was refined, resulting in the eradication of this dreaded disease.

Prior to the polio experiment just described, researchers were content to compare the health outcomes of students who were vaccinated with students in a "control group" who were not vaccinated. This approach hinged on the dubious assumption that the two groups of children were equally likely to get polio. After vaccinating hundreds of thousands of children, it was impossible for researchers to separate the effects of the vaccine from the effects of having parents willing to grant permission. This study was simply bad science that did nothing to fight polio.

By the same token, suppose you are interested in the effects of a door-to-door voter mobilization campaign, but you do not randomly assign subjects to treatment and control groups. You could foolishly compare the voting rates of the people you contacted to the voting rates of the people you did not contact. But such a comparison is meaningless because it may be that people who are available to be contacted happen to vote at higher rates than people who are not available. Dubious as this comparison is, it is what people will offer as an alternative to random assignment. Just say no, politely.

Reviving Electoral Participation

Although much of this book is directed to those who seek to sway elections, it also serves the larger purpose of offering ways to remedy low and declining rates of voter participation. As we noted at the outset, about half of the eligible electorate votes in U.S. presidential elections, and roughly one-third does so in midterm or municipal elections. Those who find these rates alarmingly low will be distressed to learn that voter turnout has declined gradually in the United States as well as in the vast majority of Western democratic countries (see box 8-4 for suggested readings on the decline in voter turnout in the United States and box 8-5 for a brief discussion of the issue). In his survey of nineteen democratic countries, Professor Martin P. Wattenberg of University of California, Irvine, found that seventeen experienced declines in turnout during the second half of the twentieth century.[13] Back in the 1950s, the United States ranked near the bottom of Western democratic countries, with 62 percent voter turnout. It continues to rank near the bottom, with 52 percent turnout.

Regardless of whether you are concerned about low voter turnout, declining voter turnout, or both, the question is what to do. Proposals abound. For simplicity, we group them into three categories. The first is massive constitutional overhaul. Institute a new electoral system that encourages minor parties so that voters will be able to choose from a wide spectrum of candidates. Introduce a system of direct electoral control over policy. Consolidate elections at all levels of government so that voters have to vote only once every two years.

Although these proposals make wonderful discussion topics for magazines and college seminars, they cannot be considered serious proposals

---

Box 8-4. Further Reading on
Voter Turnout in the United States

The following books span a range of perspectives on why American voter turnout is low or declining. Diagnoses range from the media-centered campaigns to restrictive registration laws to the lack of vigorous party competition. Prescriptions range from civic education to new journalistic norms to changes in electoral rules.

Raymond Wolfinger and Stephen J. Rosenstone, *Who Votes?* (Yale University Press, 1980).

Ruy Teixeira, *The Disappearing American Voter* (Brookings, 1992).

Stephen J. Rosenstone and John Mark Hansen, *Mobilization, Participation, and Democracy in America* (Macmillan, 1993).

Frances Fox Piven and Richard A. Cloward, *Why Americans Still Don't Vote: And Why Politicians Want It That Way* (Boston: Beacon Press, 2000).

Thomas E. Patterson, *The Vanishing Voter: Public Involvement in an Age of Uncertainty* (Alfred E. Knopf, 2002).

Martin P. Wattenberg, *Where Have All the Voters Gone?* (Harvard University Press, 2002).

---

for policy reform. Even if one were convinced that proportional representation does a better job of attracting voter participation than other electoral systems (and were willing to overlook its drawbacks), the chances that the United States will adopt such constitutional reforms are, as it were, statistically indistinguishable from zero. As for direct democracy, it is doubtful whether states that regularly present ballot initiatives and referenda to their citizens enjoy higher voter turnout as a result. And introducing direct democracy at the federal level would require a constitutional revision that fundamentally alters the dual system of representation that currently accords power on a per capita basis in the House of Representatives and on a per state basis in the Senate. Not likely any time soon.

Somewhat more realistic, if only because it is more concrete, is the idea of consolidating the election calendar. Compared with constitutional revisions, this one poses fewer risks of unintended consequences. Consolidating the election calendar would arguably increase voter turnout rates. Parties and candidates would channel their GOTV efforts toward a single campaign, the gravity of which would attract greater interest. The problem is generating the political will to impose uniformity on municipal, county, state, and federal election calendars. It is no accident that some jurisdictions choose to hold their elections at odd times; this is a calculated move by parties and interest groups seeking to diminish the influence of national election tides on their local or state elections.

A second group of proposals involves more modest policy changes related to voting procedures. Allow voters to cast ballots online. Allow ballots to be cast over a three-week period. Permit everyone who so desires to vote by mail. Create a national database that automatically reregisters people when they change address. Or institute same-day registration nationwide. One might reasonably anticipate that each of these ideas will be adopted one day, but the track record of this kind of tinkering is not impressive. A careful statistical analysis by Mary Fitzgerald, who examined the effects of changing balloting and registration rules on patterns of state turnout over time, indicates that the introduction of same-day registration rules in Idaho, Maine, Minnesota, New Hampshire, Wisconsin, and Wyoming was associated with only modest gains in turnout.[14] Permitting early and absentee balloting also boosted turnout, but again only to a small extent. The Motor Voter Law, which made the registration process easier and more widely accessible, also had small positive effects. These innovations are arguably a step in the right direction, although the specter of voting fraud looms over proposals such as same-day registration and Internet voting. But even if they could be implemented without problems, they cannot be expected to produce noticeably higher turnout rates.

The last category of proposals involves some form of voter education. Create hotlines and websites that provide free information about where to vote and what choices will appear on the ballot. Convene public debates among candidates so that voters can learn about where they stand on the issues. Encourage journalists to devote more attention to issues and less to the horse race competition between candidates. These well-intentioned proposals are steps in the right direction, but they seem unlikely to increase voter turnout. Candidate debates, like Sunday morning talk shows with politicians, typically attract appreciative but tiny audiences. Public interest websites attract little traffic. Journalists

Box 8-5. Is American Voter Turnout in Decline?

Like most trends in the realm of politics, the decline in U.S. voter turnout is a matter of dispute. After sifting through the trends in voter turnout from 1948 to 2000, political scientists Michael McDonald and Samuel Popkin concluded that turnout declined sharply during the mid-1960s and early 1970s but remained more or less constant thereafter.[1] One way to read this finding is to say, "Great. The problem hasn't gotten any worse in thirty years, so there's nothing about contemporary politics that is eroding voter turnout."

The problem with this blithe interpretation is that the overall trend in voter turnout conceals a number of conflicting currents. On the positive side of the ledger, Americans are living longer and enjoying much better health in their old age. This trend means that elderly people comprise a larger share of the electorate than they used to. It also means that seventy-five-year-olds nowadays vote at higher rates than seventy-five-year-olds a generation ago. Other positive trends include the easing of registration and absentee ballot requirements and the introduction of extended voting periods. Finally, since the 1960s, American politics has changed in ways that have brought large numbers of people into the process. The stultifying one-party South that formerly discouraged voting by African Americans and made voting in November elections a largely pointless exercise for whites now looks much more like the rest of the country in terms of the competitiveness of its elections. These and other positive trends (such as the rising average level of education in the population) lead us to expect substantial *increases* in voter turnout since the 1960s.

Offsetting these increases are two trends that diminish the overall

who write about policy debates rather than the vicissitudes of electoral fortunes find their work ignored by all but a small constituency of readers. Politics does not interest most people. It is noble but unrealistic to expect nonvoters to seek out edifying news stories, websites, or public events. In the absence of scientific evidence suggesting that these interventions actually work, our presumption is that they do not.

Our approach to raising voter turnout is rather different. Examine a range of GOTV tactics and figure out which ones are effective and cost-efficient. By demonstrating what works (and what does not), this inves-

turnout rate. The first is the replacement of personal with impersonal political appeals. One recurrent theme in this book is that the decline in face-to-face canvassing and local political activities by parties, interest groups, and nonpartisan organizations has contributed to the decline in voter turnout. The tactics that have replaced this type of political activity—direct mail, commercial phone banks, and (arguably) the mass media—are less effective in getting people to vote. It may be more than coincidence that as American-style campaign tactics insinuate themselves into countries such as Britain, their turnout rates are declining.

The advent of impersonal politics seems to have eroded the incorporation of young voters into the electoral process. Tracking the electoral participation of voters under twenty-five since 1972 (when reliable data first became available), University of Maryland researchers Peter Levine and Mark Hugo López found a gradual erosion in voter turnout rates over time.[2] In 1972 slightly more than half of those under the age of twenty-five voted, compared with less than 40 percent in 2000.

In sum, the placid voter turnout trends of the past three decades conceal the countervailing forces that lie just beneath the surface. Unless voting gets a lot easier or the elderly get a lot healthier, generational replacement will eventually drive turnout rates down.

1. Michael P. McDonald and Samuel Popkin, "The Myth of the Vanishing Voter," *American Political Science Review*, vol. 95, no. 4 (2001), pp. 963–74.
2. Peter Levine and Mark Hugo López, "Youth Turnout Has Declined by Any Measure," unpublished ms., University of Maryland, Center for Information and Research on Civic Learning and Engagement, 2002.

tigative approach provides an important signal to those engaged in electoral competition. If the market for campaign services learns from a reliable source that a particular GOTV tactic is a more cost-effective way of garnering votes, we eventually will see campaigns allocate more resources to this tactic.

We should emphasize the word "eventually" in the previous sentence. Findings from scientific studies are not likely to win converts overnight. People in politics are justifiably skeptical of what passes for research. And even if some of this skepticism could be put to rest by blue-ribbon panels executing studies of the highest quality, the problem of conflicting economic interests remains. Big money is at stake in the market for campaign services, and those who earn their livelihood in this line of work are unlikely to sit still as their product or domain of expertise is threatened. On the one hand, campaign managers profit from the services they sell, either because they hold a financial stake in firms with which the campaign subcontracts or because they expect to have an ongoing business relationship with the subcontractors. On the other hand, managers also have a financial incentive to win elections, so as to burnish their reputation en route to future consulting work. The tension between these two economic incentives comes into play when campaign managers are able to protect their reputation by employing well-accepted, profitable, but inefficient campaign tactics. In this case, they can have their cake and eat it, too, running "credible" campaigns whose activities make for handsome profits.

If we are correct in our suspicions concerning the cost-inefficiency of campaigns that rely heavily on mass media, direct mail, and conventional commercial phone banks, scientific evidence will hasten a gradual evolutionary process. Managers who run inefficient campaigns eventually will be pushed aside by those who prove more successful in electoral competition. Admittedly, the process of natural selection could take a long time to unfold. After all, there are many reasons why elections are won and lost, and the market may have difficulty identifying which tactics are truly associated with success. Perhaps that is how capital-intensive campaigning came to prominence in the first place.

Of course, a great many research questions must be answered before those seeking to sway elections will have reason to embrace GOTV activity as an especially attractive way to invest campaign dollars. The experimental research reported in this book examines only *whether* people vote, not *how* they vote. In order to show that cost-effective voter mobilization tactics are also cost-effective vote-generating tactics, we need to learn more about the extent to which persuasive communications—advertisements, phone calls, direct mail—affect voter preference. This line of experimental research is just coming into existence. Due to the constraints of the secret ballot, it is harder to study vote choice than voter turnout. Experimental researchers must either perform random assignment at the level of the voting precinct, where vote choice can be counted in the aggregate, or gather individual-level data using a post-election survey. One of the authors, Alan Gerber, has taken the lead in examining the persuasive effects of partisan direct mail and phone banks using both types of experimental research designs. The results of his studies are the subject of another book. To make a long story short, his results are quite encouraging to those hoping to find GOTV efforts to be cost-effective ways of producing votes. It turns out that minds are difficult and expensive to change, particularly in the closing days of an election campaign. Although by no means cheap or easy, mobilizing supporters may turn out to be the most cost-effective way to influence elections.

Technical Results of Door-to-Door Canvassing Experiments

his technical appendix provides brief information on and results from
each of the relevant experiments on door-to-door canvassing. Where
possible, we report experimental results estimated without covariates
(except for those covariates that reflect the strata within which randomization was performed). This approach provides the most straightforward
reading of the results, without danger of post hoc adjustment.

Prior to 1998, two randomized field experiments dealt with door-to-
door canvassing: the classic work by Samuel Eldersveld and the relatively obscure study by Roy Miller, David Bositis, and Denise Baer.[1] Both
may be credited with paving the way for later research. Indeed, these
remain among the few experimental studies to examine partisan mobilization efforts. The Eldersveld study included both partisan and nonpartisan efforts; the Miller, Bositis, and Baer study mobilized voters on
behalf of a Democratic primary candidate.

Like many seminal research articles, they suffered from some serious
limitations. The samples were far too small to detect even large mobilization effects with appreciable statistical power. In addition, Eldersveld's method of analyzing the data was biased: he lumped together the
uncontacted members of the treatment group and the control group.
Miller, Bositis, and Baer were silent on the question of how their analysis dealt with people they were unable to contact. The enormous magni-
tude of the effects they reported suggests that they may have made the
same error as Eldersveld. Despite their defects, these studies warrant the
praise due research that is far ahead of its time.

In 2000 we published an essay reporting the first large-scale randomized field experiment conducted in political science.[2] Originally conceived as a pilot study to enable us to learn the ropes of both experimental research and voter mobilization tactics, the project grew into a far-ranging study of door-to-door activity, commercial phone banks, and direct mail, each conveying alternative messages. The door-to-door effort remains the largest conducted in a single site (New Haven, Connecticut). Turnout in the control group—those not assigned to any of the three forms of voter mobilization—was 42.2 percent (N = 11,596). Of the 13,371 people assigned to receive only phone calls or mail, 43.2 percent voted. Among those assigned to be contacted solely by door-to-door canvassing, the turnout rate was 46.3 percent (N = 2,877). Among those assigned to be contacted by door-to-door canvassing as well as mail or GOTV phone calls, the turnout rate was 44.8 percent (N = 3,254).[3] Overall, since 27 percent of the treatment group lived in households where at least one person was contacted by a canvasser, the effect of the treatment on the treated was an 8.8 percentage-point increase in turnout, with a standard error of 2.6 percentage points. There were no statistically significant differences among the scripts (civic duty, neighborhood solidarity, your vote counts in a close election) in terms of their effectiveness in mobilizing voters.

Prior to the 2000 elections, we conducted two types of door-to-door canvassing experiments.[4] A study in Eugene was randomized at the individual level, while studies in Boulder and Ann Arbor were randomized at the level of city blocks. The Eugene study saw turnout increase from 62.6 percent (N = 771) to 64.6 percent (N = 1,145) among people who were registered by Youth Vote; comparable numbers for a list of voters eighteen- to twenty-nine years old drawn from the city's voter file were 55.0 percent (N = 1,007) and 59.3 percent (N = 1,003). Unfortunately, treatment-on-the-treated effects were impossible to determine because canvassers did not keep careful records of their contacts. The block-level experiments produced mixed results, with Ann Arbor showing a slight decrease and Boulder showing a slight increase; neither effect was close to statistical significance due to the relatively small number of blocks in the study. Because of uncertainties about the contact rates, none of these experiments was used to calculate the weighted averages reported below.

Although the 1998 and 2000 studies showed convincingly that face-to-face canvassing could raise turnout among those contacted, they left many questions unanswered. Would canvassing work elsewhere? Would it work in competitive as well as uncompetitive municipal races? Would

Table A-1. Results of a Door-to-Door Canvassing Experiment in Six Cities

Percent, unless otherwise noted

| Site | Control group | | Treatment group | | | |
	Turnout	Number of observations	Turnout	Number of observations	Contact rate	Treatment effect
Bridgeport	9.9	911	13.9	895	28	14.4
Columbus	8.2	1,322	9.6	1,156	14	9.7
Detroit	43.3	2,482	45.7	2,472	31	7.8
Minneapolis	25.0	1,418	26.9	1,409	19	10.1
Raleigh	29.4	2,975	29.5	1,685	45	0.2
St. Paul	37.6	1,104	42.2	1,104	32	14.4

Source: The figures in this table were calculated based on the results in tables 1 and 2 in Donald P. Green, Alan S. Gerber, and David W. Nickerson, "Getting Out the Vote in Local Elections: Results from Six Door-to-Door Canvassing Experiments," *Journal of Politics*, vol. 65, no. 4 (2003), pp. 1083–96.

it work when academics were not crafting the messages or supervising the teams of canvassers? A canvassing experiment that we conducted with David Nickerson in 2001 supplied answers to these questions for six cities; the answers were, for the most part, yes (see table A-1 for details of the results).[5] Analyzing the data for the six sites with a single regression model yielded an effect of 7.1 percentage points with a standard error of 2.2 percentage points.

In a study by David Nickerson in three of these sites (Columbus, Minneapolis, and St. Paul), canvassers randomly supplied a flyer providing information about the candidates to those who were contacted.[6] Looking only at those who were actually contacted (N = 792), he found that providing information had an effect of –0.7 percentage point (SE = 3.2). This result was not significantly different from zero.

Melissa Michelson's nonpartisan mobilization experiment extended previous work in three important directions.[7] First, her experiment shed light on how mobilization effects changed when the contact rate was raised from 30 percent (the rate typical of most other studies) to a remarkable 75 percent. Second, it showed how mobilization worked in a rural setting. The study took place in a low-turnout municipal election in a central California farming community. Third, it studied the effect of different messages by varying the campaign message between civic duty and ethnic solidarity.

Regardless of the message used, Michelson's team of Latino canvassers proved highly effective at mobilizing Latino voters, particularly Latinos registered as Democrats. For all Latinos, turnout increased from 13.8 percent (N = 298) to 18.5 percent (N = 466). For non-Latinos, turnout increased from 25.7 percent (N = 758) to 28.2 percent (N = 1,243). Canvassers contacted 73 percent of Latinos and 78 percent of non-Latinos. The scripts were not significantly different in terms of the effectiveness with which they mobilized voters. Although the overall effects were statistically significant, the effect of the treatment on the treated was somewhat smaller than in other studies (β = 4.1, SE = 2.1).

Again examining the effects of alternative messages in addition to the effects of Latino and non-Latino canvassers, Melissa Michelson and Herbert Villa focused on a sample of voters under the age of twenty-six, encouraging them to vote in the 2002 state and federal elections.[8] Turnout among Latino subjects rose from 7.2 percent (N = 1,384) to 9.3 percent (N = 1,507), and among non-Latino subjects it rose from 8.9 percent (N = 1,438) to 10.0 percent (N = 1,455). The contact rates were 51 and 39 percent, respectively. Thus the overall treatment-on-the-treated effect was 3.5 percentage points (SE = 1.6). Again, Michelson and Villa found no evidence that the content of the canvassing script made any difference.

Recruiting student canvassers to deliver nonpartisan appeals to an area with a very competitive congressional election, Elizabeth Bennion found weak effects.[9] Turnout increased from 39.5 percent (N = 1,088) to 39.7 percent (N = 1,088). Given a 41 percent contact rate, this difference implied a treatment-on-the-treated effect of just 0.5 percentage point. The small size of this experiment, however, meant that the standard error was 5.1. Thus the 95 percent confidence region extended from –10 to 10. Despite the closeness of the election, Bennion found that a civic duty appeal worked better than a close election appeal, although the difference was not statistically significant.

Unlike other studies of door-to-door canvassing, Nickerson used a placebo control design.[10] Half of those contacted were urged to recycle; the other half, to vote in the 2002 primary elections held in Denver and Minneapolis. Turnout increased from 47.7 percent (N = 279) to 56.3 percent (N = 283) among those urged to vote. Since by design the contact rate was 100 percent, the study had reasonable statistical power despite the small sample size (β = 8.6, SE = 4.2). Perhaps the most interesting aspect of this experiment was Nickerson's demonstration that turnout among roommates of persons in the treatment group was significantly higher than turnout among roommates of those in the control group.

As part of a partisan get-out-the-vote campaign sponsored by the Michigan State Democratic Party prior to the 2002 general elections, Ryan Friedrichs and David Nickerson launched a small door-to-door canvassing experiment.[11] Because the campaign focused on eighteen- to thirty-five-year-olds outside of campus towns, subjects were geographically dispersed, and contact rate was quite low, just 9 percent. Turnout increased from 43.9 percent (N = 2,458) to 45.3 percent (N = 4,854), suggesting a large effect, but subject to a great deal of uncertainty (β = 14.9, SE = 12.8).

Taking the treatment-on-the-treated effect of each study and weighting by the inverse of its sampling variance, we obtained an overall effect of 5.2 percentage points with a standard error of 1.0. This estimate implied a vote production rate of nineteen contacts per vote. This average was on the conservative side, because it did not take into account the fact that turnout rates increase more readily from base rates close to 50 percent than they do from base rates close to either 0 percent or 100 percent. If we were to exclude the Fresno study, for example, the average effect would jump to one vote for every sixteen contacts. Why would the highly successful Fresno campaign, which raised turnout significantly from 8.0 to 9.6 percent with a contact rate of 45 percent, dampen the overall effect? The reason is that, in percentage-point terms, it is harder to increase turnout at the extremes of the probability distribution.

A better way to calculate the vote production rate is to apply a nonlinear model that takes into account the difficulty of moving at the extremes of the probability distribution. We used two-stage probit to estimate nonlinear effects in each study and again weighted the results by the inverse of the sampling variance. The result was an estimated treatment-on-the-treated effect of 0.18 probit (SE = 0.03). Figure A-1 converts this result into more readily intelligible units. The X-axis is the expected voter turnout rate in the control group. The Y-axis is the number of contacts needed to produce one vote. (The reciprocal of this number reflects the number of votes per contact.) The figure suggests that it is typically harder to produce votes in very low-turnout elections or among subpopulations with very low (or very high) voting rates. When turnout is near 50 percent in the control group, votes are produced at a rate of one vote for 13.7 contacts.[12] Consistent with this pattern is the

Figure A-1. Number of Contacts Needed to Produce One Vote

Contacts per vote

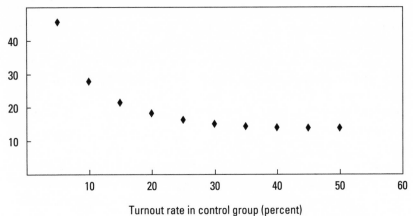

Turnout rate in control group (percent)

fact that mobilization effects in state and local elections tend to be higher among frequent voters than among infrequent voters. Voting rates among frequent voters tend to fall in the 50 percent range, whereas less than one in five infrequent voters participates in these elections.

Technical Results of Direct Mail Experiments

This technical appendix provides brief information on and results from each of the relevant experiments on direct mail. Where possible, we report experimental results estimated without covariates (except for those covariates that reflect the strata within which randomization was performed). This approach provides the most straightforward reading of the results, without danger of post hoc adjustment.

Prior to 1998, the classic work on mobilization through direct mail was by Harold Gosnell.[1] Gosnell performed two experiments in Chicago, one prior to the presidential election of 1924 and another during the following year's mayoral election. Gosnell found an effect of 1 percentage point during 1924 and 9 percentage points in 1925. The study involved thousands of Chicago residents, who were enumerated by a census-like survey. The sole defect of this study is that it did not use random assignment; instead, Gosnell assigned alternating blocks to treatment and control.

The first randomized experiments were conducted by Samuel Eldersveld in 1956 and by Roy Miller, David Bositis, and Denise Baer in 1980 (see appendix A).[2] These studies, however, were very small, involving just a few dozen subjects.

During the final weeks leading up to the 1998 election, we conducted an experiment in which registered voters in New Haven received one, two, or three pieces of nonpartisan direct mail.[3] Each batch of mail reflected one of three themes: the need to do one's civic duty, the responsibility to stand up for one's neighborhood so that politicians will take an interest in its problems, or the importance of voting in a close election. Turnout in the control group, which was not assigned to receive mail, phone calls, or door-to-door canvassing, was 42.2 percent (N = 11,596). Among those assigned to be contacted solely by mail, turnout was 42.6 percent (N = 2,550) when receiving one mailer, 43.3 percent (N = 2,699) when receiving two, and 44.6 percent (N = 2,527) when receiving three. For the sample as a whole (N = 31,098), regression estimates that controlled for the effects of phone and door-to-door canvassing put the effects of each additional mailer at 0.5 percentage point (SE = 0.3), which was significant at the 0.05 level using a one-tailed test.

The 1999 state legislative and municipal elections were the setting for a series of nonpartisan and partisan experiments that we conducted with Matthew Green.[4] In New Haven's mayoral election, nonpartisan mailings patterned after the civic duty and close election mailings used in an earlier study were sent to a random sample of the 1998 voter list. As noted in chapter 5, the blowout election offered an opportunity to see whether recipients were attending to the mailings' messages, in which case the close election appeal should have been ineffective. Results from these two manuscripts are summarized in table B-1. As predicted, the close election message had no effect, but the civic duty message performed as expected based on the 1998 results. The results suggest that returns from mailings begin to diminish after six mailings per household.

The partisan mail experiments involved a Democratic state legislative incumbent in New Jersey and a Connecticut mayoral challenger.[5] As noted in chapter 5, the New Jersey campaign divided the target population into "prime" Democrats (those with a high propensity to vote), "nonprime" Democrats and Independents, and a random sample of the list of registered voters. The mailings boosted turnout among prime Democratic households, but not among other Democrats. Turnout in the random sample rose with the number of mailings, but the effects were small given the number of mailings sent to each household. Combining all of the New Jersey samples suggests that mail did not significantly increase voter turnout. Some slight evidence for demobilization may be found in the negatively toned mayoral campaign, which sent nine mailings to each household.

In a field experiment conducted prior to the 2002 election, Janelle Wong classified Los Angeles County voters by last name into one of several Asian American groups: Chinese, Filipino, Indian, Japanese, and Korean.[6] Chinese Americans were sent one piece of nonpartisan direct mail encouraging them to vote in both English and Chinese. Other ethnic groups were sent one piece of direct mail in English. Among Chinese

Table B-1. Voter Turnout Rates, by Number of Mailings Received

Percent, unless otherwise noted

Election	None	One	Two	Three	Four	Six	Eight	Nine
				Mailings received				
1998 New Haven, nonpartisan[a]								
Civic duty message								
Turnout rate	42.2[a]	41.7	46.3	44.8	...	...	...	...
Number of observations	11,596	935	984	902	...	...	...	...
Neighborhood solidarity message								
Turnout rate	42.2[a]	42.0	44.4	43.9	...	...	...	...
Number of observations	11,596	810	872	795	...	...	...	...
Close election message								
Turnout rate	42.2[a]	44.2	38.8	44.9	...	...	...	...
Number of observations	11,596	805	843	830	...	...	...	...
1999 New Haven, nonpartisan[b]								
Civic duty message								
Turnout rate	39.3[b]	...	39.0	...	44.9	46.0	42.9	...
Number of observations	21,906	...	561	...	272	289	546	...
Close election message								
Turnout rate	39.3[b]	...	35.1	...	37.4	39.2	39.7	...
Number of observations	21,096	...	547	...	262	286	531	...
1999 New Jersey, partisan								
Prime Democrats								
Turnout rate	63.7	...	...	...	65.6	...	...	...
Number of observations	1,203	...	...	...	9,955	...	...	...
Other Democrats and Independents								
Turnout rate	54.2	...	...	...	54.2	...	...	...
Number of observations	1,925	...	...	...	17,816	...	...	...
Republicans and low-turnout Independents								
Turnout rate	23.1	...	...	...	23.5	24.1	...	...
Number of observations	1,863	...	...	...	990	1,447	...	...
1999 Connecticut mayoral, partisan with negative tone								
Turnout rate	56.1	...	...	...	...	...	...	55.0
Number of observations	2,155	...	...	...	...	...	...	17,693
2002 Pennsylvania, partisan								
Prime Republicans								
Turnout rate	89.0	90.6	...	...	...	...	...	...
Number of observations	819	7,224	...	...	...	...	...	...
Other Republicans								
Turnout rate	63.6	...	65.1	...	...	...	...	...
Number of observations	1,306	...	9,301	...	...	...	...	...
Independents and Democrats								
Turnout rate	73.8	...	...	73.0	...	...	...	...
Number of observations	4,606	...	...	30,727	...	...	...	...

... Not applicable.

a. The control group is the same for all three New Haven experiments in 1998.

b. The control group is the same for both New Haven experiments in 1999.

Americans, turnout in the control group was 29.0 percent (2,924); the treatment group turned out at a rate of 31.7 percent (1,137). Among other Asian groups, the control group voted at a rate of 38.5 percent (N = 5,802), compared with the treatment group rate of 39.4 percent (N = 2,095). When combined, the two samples suggest a treatment effect of 1.4 percentage points (SE = 1.0).

A report by Donald Green grew out of a randomized evaluation of the NAACP National Voter Fund's direct mail and phone bank efforts during the final weeks of the 2000 election campaign.[7] A small proportion of the target lists in Florida, Georgia, Michigan, Missouri, Ohio, Pennsylvania, New Jersey, New York, and Virginia was assigned to a control group. The target population varied from state to state but, on the whole, consisted of people living in neighborhoods with a high density of African Americans. Those with very high or very low propensities to vote were called; others received mail and were called. Although the sample was very large (for one-voter households: N = 16,712 for the control group and N = 963,496 for the treatment group), the experiment was marred by low contact rates. Many of those eligible to receive mail were never sent it. The two to three experimental mailings had no effect regardless of whether subjects had already received direct mail from the National Voter Fund ($\beta = -0.2$, SE = 0.8).

Alan Gerber examined the turnout effects of direct mail sent by a Republican incumbent member of Congress in the course of a primary election campaign and a general election campaign.[8] The primary featured a credible challenger; the general election was won decisively. Randomization was performed at the precinct level. In the Republican primary election, 239 precincts were targeted for a two-piece direct mail campaign; five were placed in a control group that received no mail. Regression analysis that controlled for factors such as past history of turnout indicated that the mail increased turnout in the treatment precincts by 2.7 percentage points, with a 1.7 percentage-point standard error. The general election campaign excluded households in which all members were Democrats who voted in primaries. The remaining households were categorized as prime Republicans, nonprime Republicans, and others, depending on party registration and the number of times they voted in primary elections. The three groups were sent one, two, and three mailings, respectively. Because randomization occurred at the precinct level, adjustments were made to the standard errors of each experimental comparison when combining the estimates with those of other partisan mail experiments. See table B-1.

Finally, in two reports Ricardo Ramírez and his colleagues examined the effects of a multisite nonpartisan campaign designed to mobilize Latino voters in low-voting precincts.[9] Lists of registered voters with Latino surnames were obtained for Los Angeles County, Orange County (California), Houston, New Mexico, and Colorado. The treatments consisted of robo phone calls, direct mail, and (in Los Angeles and Orange counties only) live phone calls from local, volunteer phone banks. Each of these treatments was administered separately and in combinations, using a factorial design. The mailers all used bilingual text on multicolor, folding glossy paper. The number of mailers varied across sites from two to four. Based on 349,293 observations, the results indicated that each mailing had an effect of 0.04 percentage point (SE = 0.05). Excluding those observations that were assigned to multiple treatments in order to estimate the effect of each treatment in isolation yielded estimates that were statistically quite similar: each mailing had an effect of 0.04 percentage point (SE = 0.06, N = 146,147).

Technical Results of Phone Calling Experiments

This technical appendix provides brief information on and results from each of the relevant experiments on phone calling. Where possible, we report experimental results estimated without covariates (except for those covariates that reflect the strata within which randomization was performed). This approach provides the most straightforward reading of the results, without danger of post hoc adjustment.

Three early studies of the effects of phone canvassing were conducted by Samuel Eldersveld in 1956, Roy Miller, David Bositis, and Denise Baer in 1981, and William Adams and Dennis Smith in 1980.[1] As noted in appendix A, the former two studies involved very small samples. The first phone bank experiment to be performed on a scale large enough to produce informative results was conducted by Adams and Smith, who examined the consequences of a commercial phone bank campaign conducted on behalf of a candidate running in a Washington, D.C., special election. Using a post-election survey, Adams and Smith found the phone calls to have no effect on candidate preference. They did, however, report a large mobilization effect. Unfortunately, like Eldersveld, they lumped together the noncontacted members of the treatment group and the control group. Recalculating their estimates to correct this problem indicates that 23.8 percent of the control group voted (N = 1,325), compared with 29.6 percent of the treatment group (N = 1,325), 72 percent of whom were contacted. This pattern yields a treatment-on-the-treated effect of 8.1 percentage points (SE = 2.4), which is by far the largest effect to emerge from any commercial phone bank experiment.

During the weekend prior to the 1998 federal midterm election, we examined the effects of brief calls conducted by a commercial phone bank to New Haven residents living outside the ward containing the Yale University campus.[2] The calls were nonpartisan in nature. Each respondent received one of three scripts emphasizing either civic duty, the importance of voting so that politicians have an incentive to listen to one's neighborhood, or the closeness of the election. None of the GOTV scripts increased turnout to a significant degree. The control group, which was excluded from all forms of attempted mobilization, voted at a rate of 42.2 percent (N = 11,596); those in the group slated for phone calls (and no other treatments) voted at a rate of 41.8 percent (N = 846), with 33 percent living in a household where at least one person was contacted. Phone calls also had no effect on those who were randomly assigned to be mobilized either by mail or by face-to-face canvassing. Those excluded from the phone treatment voted at a rate of 44.3 percent (N = 12,506), while those in the treatment group, 34 percent of whom lived in a household where at least one person was contacted, voted at a rate of 43.4 percent (N = 6,150). Analyzing the sample as a whole and all of the treatments simultaneously yielded an estimated effect of –1.6 percentage points (SE = 2.4, correcting for within-household correlation of individuals). There were no significant differences among the three scripts in terms of the effectiveness with which they mobilized voters.

Another study conducted in 1998 was based on the same phone bank, scripts, and election as our New Haven study but drew its sample from the neighboring city of West Haven.[3] Phone canvassing was the sole treatment used to mobilize voters. Again, no differences were found in the mobilizing effects of alternative scripts. The estimated effects of GOTV calls were also weakly negative. The control group (N = 7,137) voted at a rate of 51.5 percent, compared with 51.1 percent among those assigned to receive a GOTV phone call (N = 7,724). Those assigned to receive a call asking them to donate blood (N = 3,005) voted at a rate of 50.9 percent. We can improve the statistical efficiency of this comparison by considering only those people whose phone numbers were supplied to the phone bank.[4] Among this subsample, voting rates were 57.3 percent for the blood donation group (N = 2,089) and 57.0 percent for the GOTV group (N = 5,271). When the effects of GOTV and blood donation calls were estimated jointly using the full sample (N = 17,866), GOTV calls were found to have a statistically insignificant effect of –0.9 percentage point (robust SE = 2.1) on those who received them. Again, there were no significant differences across scripts.

Table C-1. Results of a Volunteer
Phone-Bank Experiment in Four Cities

Percent, unless otherwise noted

Site	Control group		Treatment group		
	Turnout	Number of obser- vations	Turnout	Number of obser- ations	Contact rate[a]
List of persons registered to vote by Youth Vote					
Albany	74.2	318	78.0	804	62
Stony Brook	70.6	279	78.8	680	89
Boulder	62.6	441	64.9	653	72
Eugene	61.2	497	61.7	705	74
Targeted list of registered voters eighteen to thirty years of age[b]					
Boulder	28.0	1,175	28.2	1,143	35
Eugene	55.0	1,007	57.6	953	49

Source: David W. Nickerson, "Phone Calls Can Increase Turnout: Evidence from Six Field Experiments," unpublished ms., Yale University, Institution for Social and Policy Studies, 2004.
a. Counts messages left with roommates as contacts.
b. Supplied by a commercial vendor.

During the 2000 general election campaign, we conducted random-ized experiments designed to evaluate the volunteer phone bank efforts in Albany, Stony Brook, Boulder, and Eugene, all of which were aimed at young voters.[5] Volunteers in Albany and Stony Brook called only those people who had been registered to vote by Youth Vote earlier in the cam-paign. Volunteers in Boulder and Eugene called two lists of names: those people who were registered by Youth Vote and a random sample of reg-istered voters eighteen to thirty years of age (see table C-1 for detailed results). Given the results in Boulder and Eugene, it does not appear that phone banks are more successful when mobilizing people who were reg-istered by an affiliated campaign. Taking all of the results and weighting by the inverse of the sampling variances yielded an overall effect of 4.5 percentage points with a standard error of 1.7.

This study also reported the results of a small experiment conducted at Colorado State University, in which young voters were randomly called once or twice with GOTV messages alone or with GOTV messages and information about the location of their polling place. Compared with a single call, two calls did not increase turnout ($\beta = -0.4$, SE = 2.4). Polling place information increased turnout, but not significantly ($\beta = 3.1$, SE = 3.1).

As part of the Youth Vote Coalition's 2001 GOTV campaign, which attempted to mobilize voters of all ages, David Nickerson conducted three phone bank studies.[6] Two live calling campaigns by volunteers were conducted in Boston and Seattle. The control group in Boston voted at a rate of 54.5 percent (N = 5,846), compared with 56.1 percent in the treatment group (N = 1,209). The treatment-on-the-treated effect was 2.9 percentage points (SE = 2.8). Seattle's calls appear to have had no effect, but the margin of error is large because less than 10 percent of the treatment group was reached. Turnout in the control group (N = 33,020) was the same as in the treatment group (N = 10,757), 64.7 percent. The estimated treatment-on-treated effect was 0.1 (SE = 5.5). Some who were contacted were randomly supplied with polling information, which boosted their turnout 1.6 percentage points; however, the standard error of this coefficient was 2.9. Seattle was also the site for a study of robo calls, in which the voting rate was 64.9 percent in the control group (N = 22,226) and 64.4 percent in the treatment group (N = 10,000).

In 2002 an enormous experiment targeted residents of Iowa and Michigan with working phone numbers.[7] The congressional districts of each state were divided into "competitive" and "uncompetitive" strata. Within each stratum, households containing one or two registered voters were randomly assigned to treatment and control groups. Only one type of treatment was used: GOTV phone calls, using a short "civic duty" script. Just one representative from each household was assigned to treatment or control; the other voter was ignored for purposes of calling and statistical analysis. A total of 60,000 individuals were assigned to be called by two commercial phone banks; the corresponding control group contained 1,846,885 individuals.

The 2002 results turned out to be quite similar to the 1998 findings. The estimated effect of the treatment on the treated, controlling for the two design strata (state and competitiveness), was 0.36 percentage point. Due to the massive sample size, the standard error of this estimate was just 0.5 percentage point, which means that the 95 percent confidence region extended from –0.6 to 1.3. The results changed only trivially when controls were introduced for past voting behavior, age, or other covariates. There were no significant interactions across state, competitiveness stratum, or phone bank.

In a study conducted with David Nickerson, we examined the effects of several GOTV phone bank efforts designed to mobilize voters between eighteen and twenty-six years of age.[8] The largest experiment involved a national commercial phone bank that, as explained in chapter 6, was paid a premium to deliver a longer script with greater supervision of the callers. Within the more than a dozen metropolitan areas in the study, 27,142 people were assigned to the control group, and 54,804 were assigned to the treatment group. Over a four-week calling period, during which individuals were called between one and four times, the phone bank contacted at least once approximately 39 percent of the voters they sought to reach; during the last week, this rate was 26 percent, which is somewhat lower than the other commercial phone banks. Calls during the first three weeks of the phone bank campaign had no apparent effect on turnout, but the last week's calls significantly increased voter participation: successful contact with voters increased turnout 5.1 percentage points (SE = 2.1).

The closely supervised local commercial phone bank in the Denver area, which used a lenghty script, also generated impressive results. In this experiment, 2,424 people were in the control group. Of the 4,849 people in the treatment group, 31 percent were successfully contacted. Its calls increased turnout 5.6 percentage points (SE = 3.0, significant at $p < 0.05$).

Phone banks that relied on temps and other part-time workers produced relatively weak results. Despite contacting 46 percent of the 49,045 people in the treatment group (the control group numbered 27,142 people, the same as above), these phone banks increased turnout just 0.5 percentage point (SE = 0.6). When we restricted our attention to the subjects who were not also called by the commercial phone bank, this effect rose to 1.7 percentage points with a 0.9 percentage-point standard error.

A study reported by both Ryan Friedrichs and David Nickerson gauged the effectiveness of partisan canvassing prior to the 2002 election.[9] The sample consisted of voters eighteen to thirty-five years old who did not have a history of Republican voter registration and who resided in one of six state house districts. The calls were conducted by volunteers working for the Michigan Democratic Party. The control group consisted of 5,631 people; the treatment group consisted of 10,550, of whom 50 percent were contacted. The effect of the treatment on the treated was 3.2 percentage points, with a standard error of 1.7 percentage points.

John McNulty reported on a phone bank campaign conducted on behalf of the Coalition for San Francisco Neighborhoods in opposition to

Proposition D, a municipal ballot issue that would have allowed the Public Utilities Commission to raise revenue bonds without voter approval.[10] A commercial phone bank targeted voters thought to be sympathetic to the "No on D" effort. Turnout in the control group was 57.4 percent (N = 1,485), as opposed to 57.6 percent in the treatment group (N = 28,479), of whom 50 percent were contacted. The estimated treatment-on-the-treated effect was 0.5 percentage point (SE = 2.6).

A remarkable phone canvassing campaign, conducted by Janelle Wong, used a mixture of English-speaking and bilingual callers to contact Los Angeles County voters classified by last name into one of several Asian American groups: Chinese, Filipino, Indian, Japanese, and Korean. Volunteer callers read a very brief script reminding listeners of the upcoming election.[11] Among Chinese Americans, turnout in the control group was 29.0 percent (N = 2,924) as compared to 31.2 percent in the treatment group (N = 1,484), of whom 35 percent were contacted. Overall, however, the effects were weaker. For the entire sample, the estimated treatment-on-the-treated effect was 2.0 percentage points (SE = 2.4).

A report by Donald Green grew out of a randomized evaluation of the NAACP National Voter Fund's direct mail and phone bank efforts during the final weeks of the 2000 election campaign.[12] A small proportion of the target lists in Florida, Georgia, Michigan, Missouri, Ohio, Pennsylvania, New Jersey, New York, and Virginia was assigned to a control group. The target population varied from state to state but typically consisted of people living in neighborhoods with a high density of African Americans. Subjects in the phone treatment group were called twice in October by a commercial phone bank, twice during the weekend before the election with robo calls, and once on election day with a live reminder phone call. Those with very high or very low propensities to vote were called but not mailed; the rest of the population received mail and was called. Although the sample was very large (for one-voter households, N = 16,712 for the control group and N = 963,496 for the treatment group), the experiment was marred by low contact rates. Many of those eligible to be called were never called; some of those in the control group were called by mistake. Adjusting for these problems yielded estimates suggesting that assignment to the phone campaign raised turnout 2.3 percentage points with a 2.3 percentage-point standard error. Restricting the sample to those with listed phone numbers reduces this intent-to-treat estimate to 0.4 (SE = 2.2).

The effects of a multisite nonpartisan campaign designed to mobilize Latino voters in low-voting precincts were the subject of reports by

Ricardo Ramírez and by Ramírez, Gerber, and Green.[13] Lists of registered voters with Latino surnames were obtained for Los Angeles County, Orange County (California), Houston, New Mexico, and Colorado. The treatments consisted of robo phone calls, direct mail, and (in Los Angeles and Orange counties only) live phone calls from local, volunteer phone banks. Each of these treatments was administered separately and in combinations, using a factorial design. Those in the group receiving robo calls were called twice, each time in Spanish (except for Colorado residents, who received one call in English and another in Spanish). The mailers all used bilingual text on multicolor, folding glossy paper. The number of mailers varied across sites from two to four. Using 2SLS, we regressed votes on actual contact (or messages left on answering machines) by robo call, the number of mailings sent, contact by live call, and dummy variables marking each site. The instrumental variables were site dummies, random assignment to live or robo calls, and assigned number of mailings. The results based on 368,844 observations indicate that live calls had an effect of 4.6 percentage points (SE = 1.8), a pair of robo calls had an effect of 0.04 percentage point (SE = 0.20), and each mailing had an effect of 0.04 percentage point (SE = 0.05). Excluding those observations that were assigned to multiple treatments in order to estimate the effect of each treatment in isolation yielded estimates that were statistically quite similar. Based on a sample size of 166,000, the regression analysis suggested that live calls had an effect of 4.5 percentage points (SE = 4.4), a pair of robo calls had an effect of 0.08 percentage point (SE = 0.33), and each mailing had an effect of 0.04 percentage point (SE = 0.06).

In order to synthesize the results of all of these phone call studies, we weighted each estimate by its precision (the inverse of its sampling variance). These estimates were grouped into (1) commercial phone banks with brief scripts (New Haven, West Haven, Iowa, Michigan, and San Francisco Ballot Measure), (2) commercial phone banks with longer scripts and better training (Youth Vote 2002 National Phone Bank, Youth Vote 2002 Boulder-Denver Phone Bank), and (3) volunteer efforts (Youth Vote 2000, Youth Vote 2001, Youth Vote 2002, NALEO 2002, Asian Americans 2002, Michigan Democrats). We did not include the NAACP National Voter Fund's results in these calculations, although doing so would not have appreciably affected the results.

Because the base rates for voting tended to fall in the 30–70 percent range (low voting rates of the kind seen in some door-to-door canvassing efforts do not occur in phone experiments, as the samples are restricted to persons with working phone numbers), applying nonlinear models to these data has very little effect on overall results. The cumulative estimated effect of commercial phone banks with brief scripts was 0.2 percentage point (SE = 0.5); for commercial phone banks with longer scripts, the estimated effect was 5.3 percentage points (SE = 1.7), although this result should be read with some caution because it throws out phone calls conducted prior to the last week of the campaign, which turned out to be ineffective. The cumulative estimated effect for volunteer phone banks was 2.7 percentage points (SE = 0.6). Excluding the Youth Vote 2002 phone banks, which used paid staff, this estimate climbed to 3.6 (SE = 0.9).

Notes

Chapter One

1. This pattern is demonstrated in Stephen D. Ansolabehere, Alan Gerber, and James M. Snyder Jr., "Equal Votes, Equal Money: Court-Ordered Redistricting and Public Expenditures in the American States," *American Political Science Review,* vol. 96, no. 4 (2002), pp. 767–78.

2. Hal Malchow, *The New Political Marketing* (Washington: Campaigns and Elections Magazine, 2003), pp. 281–82.

Chapter Two

1. Ron Faucheux, ed., *The Road to Victory 2000* (Dubuque, Iowa: Kendall-Hunt, 1998), p. 620.

2. Democratic National Committee, *GOTV* (Washington, 1995), p. 28.

3. Republican National Committee, *State Legislative and Local Campaign Manual* (Washington, 2000), pp. 167, 189.

4. This advice was found at the Humboldt County California Green Party website: www.arcata.com/green [June 15, 2003].

5. Results from the Steen and Lapinski studies were unavailable as this book went to press.

Chapter Three

1. For purposes of this calculation (and throughout the book), we define contact to include speaking to a voter's housemate. If a canvasser speaks to eight

people at different addresses and each household contains an average of 1.5 voters, we count that as twelve contacts.

2. In 2000 we also conducted experiments in which canvassers trolling neighborhoods surrounding the University of Colorado and University of Michigan were assigned to streets rather than to individuals.

3. Melissa R. Michelson, "Getting Out the Latino Vote: How Door-to-Door Canvassing Influences Voter Turnout in Rural Central California," *Political Behavior,* vol. 25, no. 3 (2003), pp. 247–63; Melissa R. Michelson and Herbert Villa Jr., "Mobilizing the Latino Youth Vote," paper presented at the annual meeting of the Western Political Science Association, Denver, 2003; Alan S. Gerber and Donald P. Green, "The Effects of Canvassing, Direct Mail, and Telephone Contact on Voter Turnout: A Field Experiment," *American Political Science Review,* vol. 94, no. 3 (2000), pp. 653–63; Elizabeth A. Bennion, "Message, Context, and Turnout: A Voter Mobilization Field Experiment," paper presented at the annual meeting of the Midwest Political Science Association, Chicago, 2003.

4. Donald P. Green and Alan S. Gerber, "Getting Out the Youth Vote: Results from Randomized Field Experiments," unpublished ms., Yale University, Institution for Social and Policy Studies, 2001; Donald P. Green, Alan S. Gerber, and David W. Nickerson, "Getting Out the Vote in Local Elections: Results from Six Door-to-Door Canvassing Experiments," *Journal of Politics,* vol. 65, no. 4 (2003), pp. 1083–96; David W. Nickerson, "Memo on the Effectiveness of Messages Used in Door-to-Door Canvassing Prior to the 2001 Elections," unpublished ms., Yale University, Institution for Social and Policy Studies, 2002.

5. Ryan Friedrichs, "Mobilizing 18–35-Year-Old Voters: An Analysis of the Michigan Democratic Party's 2002 Youth Coordinated Campaign," unpublished thesis, Harvard University, John F. Kennedy School of Government, 2003; David W. Nickerson, "Memo Concerning Michigan Democratic Mobilization Experiment," unpublished ms., Yale University, Institution for Social and Policy Studies, 2003.

6. For an explanation of statistical significance, please see www.research.yale.edu/vote.

7. David W. Nickerson, "Measuring Interpersonal Influence," Ph.D. diss., Yale University, Department of Political Science, to be completed in 2004.

Chapter Four

1. Ryan Friedrichs, "Mobilizing 18–35-Year-Old Voters: An Analysis of the Michigan Democratic Party's 2002 Youth Coordinated Campaign," unpublished thesis, Harvard University, John F. Kennedy School of Government, 2003; David W. Nickerson, "Memo Concerning Michigan Democratic Mobilization Experiment," unpublished ms., Yale University, Institution for Social and Policy Studies, 2003.

2. Alan S. Gerber and Donald P. Green, "The Effect of a Nonpartisan Get-Out-the-Vote Drive: An Experimental Study of Leafleting," *Journal of Politics,* vol. 62, no. 3 (2000), pp. 846–57.

Chapter Five

1. *California Prolife Council PAC* v. *Fair Political Practices Commission*, No. 9-6-01965, Federal District Court for the Eastern District of California, vol. 6, at 945. Transcript, July 19, 2000.

2. The U.S. Postal Service website (www.usps.gov) presents a complete rundown on mailing sizes and weights.

3. Harold F. Gosnell, *Getting-Out-the-Vote: An Experiment in the Stimulation of Voting* (University of Chicago Press, 1927).

4. Alan S. Gerber and Donald P. Green, "The Effects of Canvassing, Direct Mail, and Telephone Contact on Voter Turnout: A Field Experiment," *American Political Science Review*, vol. 94, no. 3 (2000), pp. 653–63.

5. Alan S. Gerber, Donald P. Green, and Matthew N. Green, "Direct Mail and Voter Turnout: Results from Seven Randomized Field Experiments," unpublished ms., Yale University, Institution for Social and Policy Studies, 2000.

6. Donald P. Green, "Mobilizing African-American Voters Using Direct Mail and Commercial Phone Banks: A Field Experiment," *Political Research Quarterly* (forthcoming, 2004).

7. Alan S. Gerber, Donald P. Green, and Matthew N. Green, "The Effects of Partisan Direct Mail on Voter Turnout," *Electoral Studies*, vol. 22 (2003), pp. 563–79.

8. See Alan S. Gerber, "Does Campaign Spending Work?" *American Behavioral Scientist*, vol. 47 (2004), pp. 541–74.

9. Janelle Wong, "Getting Out the Vote among Asian Americans in Los Angeles County: A Field Experiment," paper presented at the annual meeting of the American Political Science Association, Philadelphia, August 28–31, 2003.

10. Ricardo Ramírez, "Where No Party Has Gone Before . . . Non-Partisan Latino Voter Mobilization and Issues of Contactability," paper prepared for the Nation of Immigrants conference, University of California, Berkeley, Institute of Governmental Studies, May 2–3, 2003; Ricardo Ramírez, Alan S. Gerber, and Donald P. Green, "An Evaluation of NALEO's 2002 Voter Mobilization Campaign," unpublished ms., Yale University, Institution for Social and Policy Studies, 2003.

Chapter Six

1. Alan S. Gerber and Donald P. Green, "The Effects of Canvassing, Direct Mail, and Telephone Contact on Voter Turnout: A Field Experiment," *American Political Science Review*, vol. 94, no. 3 (2000), pp. 653–63; Alan S. Gerber and Donald P. Green, "Do Phone Calls Increase Voter Turnout? A Field Experiment," *Public Opinion Quarterly*, vol. 65 (2001), pp. 75–85.

2. Kevin Arceneaux, Alan S. Gerber, and Donald P. Green, "Two Large-Scale Field Experiments Using Phone Calls to Get Out the Vote: Comparing Experimental and Matching Methods," unpublished ms., Yale University, Institution for Social and Policy Studies, 2003.

3. John E. McNulty, "Partisan Get-Out-the-Vote Drives and Turnout," paper presented at the annual meeting of the Midwest Political Science Association, Chicago, April 3–6, 2003.

4. Donald P. Green, Alan S. Gerber, and David W. Nickerson, "The Challenge of Bringing Voter Mobilization 'To Scale': An Evaluation of Youth Vote's 2002 Phone Banking Campaigns," unpublished ms., Yale University, Institution for Social and Policy Studies, 2003.

5. Ryan Friedrichs, "Mobilizing 18–35-Year-Old Voters: An Analysis of the Michigan Democratic Party's 2002 Youth Coordinated Campaign," unpublished thesis, Harvard University, John F. Kennedy School of Government, 2003.

6. Ricardo Ramírez, Alan S. Gerber, and Donald P. Green, "An Evaluation of NALEO's 2002 Voter Mobilization Campaign," unpublished ms., Yale University, Institution for Social and Policy Studies, 2003.

7. Janelle Wong, "Getting Out the Vote among Asian Americans in Los Angeles County: A Field Experiment," paper presented at the annual meeting of the American Political Science Association, Philadelphia, August 28–31, 2003.

Chapter Seven

1. Pew Internet and American Life Project, "The Internet News Audience Goes Ordinary," unpublished ms., Pew Research Center for People and the Press, 1999.

2. National Telecommunications and Information Administration, *A Nation Online: How Americans Are Expanding Their Use of the Internet* (February 2002).

3. John Anthony Phillips, "Using E-Mail to Mobilize Young Voters: A Field Experiment," unpublished ms., Yale University, May 21, 2001.

Chapter Eight

1. Anthony G. Greenwald, Catherine G. Carnot, Rebecca Beach, and Barbara Young, "Increasing Voting Behavior by Asking People If They Expect to Vote," *Journal of Applied Psychology*, vol. 72 (May 1987), pp. 315–18.

2. Roy E. Miller, David A. Bositis, and Denise L. Baer, "Stimulating Voter Turnout in a Primary: Field Experiment with a Precinct Committeeman," *International Political Science Review*, vol. 2, no. 4 (1981), table 1.

3. Jennifer K. Smith, Alan S. Gerber, and Anton Orlich, "Self-Prophecy Effects and Voter Turnout: An Experimental Replication," *Political Psychology*, vol. 24, no. 3 (2003), pp. 594–604.

4. Christopher Mann, "Getting Preelection Surveys Right: The Effects of Advance Letters on Preelection Forecasting," paper presented at the annual conference of the American Association for Public Opinion Research, Nashville, May 2003.

5. For further discussion and evidence on this point, see Alan S. Gerber, Donald P. Green, and David Nickerson, "Testing for Publication Bias in Political Science," *Political Analysis*, vol. 9, no. 4 (2001), pp. 385–92.

6. Elizabeth M. Addonizio, David B. Ogle, and Beth I. Weinberger, "Voting Booth Familiarity: Project to Increase Voter Turnout among Eighteen-Year-

Olds," unpublished ms., Yale University, Institution for Social and Policy Studies, 2003.

7. Alan S. Gerber, Donald P. Green, and Ron Shachar, "Voting May Be Habit Forming: Evidence from a Randomized Field Experiment," *American Journal of Political Science,* vol. 47, no. 3 (2003), pp. 540–50.

8. Melissa R. Michelson, "Dos Palos Revisited: Testing the Lasting Effects of Voter Mobilization," paper presented at the annual meeting of the Midwest Political Science Association, Chicago, April 3–6, 2003; David W. Nickerson, "Habit Formation from the 2001 YouthVote Experiments," ISPS Working Paper (Yale University, Institution for Social and Policy Studies, December 15, 2003); David W. Nickerson, "Voter Contagion Phone Mobilization Experiment," ISPS Working Paper (Yale University, Institution for Social and Policy Studies, December 16, 2003); David W. Nickerson, "Habit Formation from 2002 Placebo Controlled Experiments," ISPS Working Paper (Yale University, Institution for Social and Policy Studies, December 16, 2003). Taken together, these studies imply that each vote in the current election generates an additional 32.5 votes in the subsequent election (SE = 12.4, p < 0.05).

9. The closest approximation to a field experiment in this area may be found in Sandra J. Ball-Rokeach, Milton Rokeach, and Joel W. Grube, *The Great American Values Test: Influencing Behavior and Belief through Television* (New York: Free Press, 1984).

10. Joshua D. Clinton and John S. Lapinski, "'Targeted' Advertising and Voter Turnout: An Experimental Study of the 2000 Presidential Election," *Journal of Politics,* vol. 66, no. 1 (forthcoming, 2004). See also Lynn Vavreck, "Campaign Advertising Effectiveness: Experimental versus Observational Tests," paper prepared for presentation at the ninety-ninth meeting of the American Political Science Association, Philadelphia, 2003.

11. Note that all the names you attempted belong in the treatment group, even those who could not be reached when called.

12. Paul Meier, "The Biggest Public Health Experiment Ever: The 1954 Field Trial of the Salk Poliomyelitis Vaccine," in Judith M. Tanur, Richard S. Pieters, and Frederick Mosteller, eds., *Statistics: A Guide to the Unknown,* 3d ed. (Pacific Grove, Calif.: Wadsworth and Brooks, 1989), pp. 3–14.

13. Martin P. Wattenberg, "The Decline of Party Mobilization," in Russell J. Dalton and Martin P. Wattenberg, eds., *Partisans without Parties: Political Change in Advanced Industrial Democracies,* pp. 64–76 (New York: Oxford University Press, 2000).

14. Mary Fitzgerald, "The Impact of Alternative Voting Methods on Electoral Participation in the U.S.," unpublished ms., James Madison University, December 22, 2002.

Appendix A

1. Samuel J. Eldersveld, "Experimental Propaganda Techniques and Voting Behavior," *American Political Science Review,* vol. 50 (March 1956), pp. 154–65; Roy E. Miller, David A. Bositis, and Denise L. Baer, "Stimulating Voter

Turnout in a Primary: Field Experiment with a Precinct Committeeman," *International Political Science Review,* vol. 2, no. 4 (1981), pp. 445–60.

2. Alan S. Gerber and Donald P. Green, "The Effects of Canvassing, Direct Mail, and Telephone Contact on Voter Turnout: A Field Experiment," *American Political Science Review,* vol. 94, no. 3 (2000), pp. 653–63.

3. These results are very slightly different from those reported in the article, given some post-publication corrections to the data.

4. Donald P. Green and Alan S. Gerber, "Getting Out the Youth Vote: Results from Randomized Field Experiments," unpublished ms., Yale University, Institution for Social and Policy Studies, 2001.

5. Donald P. Green, Alan S. Gerber, and David W. Nickerson, "Getting Out the Vote in Local Elections: Results from Six Door-to-Door Canvassing Experiments," *Journal of Politics,* vol. 65, no. 4 (2003), pp. 1083–96.

6. David W. Nickerson, "Memo on the Effectiveness of Messages Used in Door-to-Door Canvassing Prior to the 2001 Elections," unpublished ms., Yale University, Institution for Social and Policy Studies, 2002.

7. Melissa R. Michelson, "Getting Out the Latino Vote: How Door-to-Door Canvassing Influences Voter Turnout in Rural Central California," *Political Behavior,* vol. 25, no. 3 (2003), pp. 247–63.

8. Melissa R. Michelson and Herbert Villa Jr., "Mobilizing the Latino Youth Vote," paper presented at the annual meeting of the Western Political Science Association, Denver, Colo., 2003.

9. Elizabeth A. Bennion, "Message, Context, and Turnout: A Voter Mobilization Field Experiment," paper presented at the annual meeting of the Midwest Political Science Association, Chicago, 2003.

10. David W. Nickerson, "Measuring Interpersonal Influence," Ph.D. diss., Yale University, Department of Political Science, to be completed in 2004.

11. Ryan Friedrichs, "Mobilizing 18–35-Year-Old Voters: An Analysis of the Michigan Democratic Party's 2002 Youth Coordinated Campaign," unpublished thesis, Harvard University, John F. Kennedy School of Government, 2003; David W. Nickerson, "Memo Concerning Michigan Democratic Mobilization Experiment," unpublished ms., Yale University, Institution for Social and Policy Studies, 2003.

12. This figure does not include the effects of spillover, which occurs when people are contacted either inadvertently or indirectly through conversation within households. See Nickerson, "Measuring Interpersonal Influence."

Appendix B

1. Harold F. Gosnell, *Getting-Out-the-Vote: An Experiment in the Stimulation of Voting* (University of Chicago Press, 1927).

2. Samuel J. Eldersveld, "Experimental Propaganda Techniques and Voting Behavior," *American Political Science Review,* vol. 50 (March 1956), pp. 154–65; Roy E. Miller, David A. Bositis, and Denise L. Baer, "Stimulating Voter Turnout in a Primary: Field Experiment with a Precinct Committeeman," *International Political Science Review,* vol. 2, no. 4 (1981), pp. 445–60.

3. Alan S. Gerber and Donald P. Green, "The Effects of Canvassing, Direct

Mail, and Telephone Contact on Voter Turnout: A Field Experiment," *American Political Science Review,* vol. 94, no. 3 (2000), pp. 653–63.

4. Alan S. Gerber, Donald P. Green, and Matthew N. Green, "Direct Mail and Voter Turnout: Results from Seven Randomized Field Experiments," unpublished ms., Yale University, Institution for Social and Policy Studies, 2000.

5. Alan S. Gerber, Donald P. Green, and Matthew N. Green, "The Effects of Partisan Direct Mail on Voter Turnout," *Electoral Studies,* vol. 22 (2003), pp. 563–79.

6. Janelle Wong, "Getting out the Vote among Asian Americans in Los Angeles County: A Field Experiment," paper presented at the annual meeting of the American Political Science Association, Philadelphia, August 28–31, 2003.

7. Donald P. Green, "Mobilizing African-American Voters Using Direct Mail and Commercial Phone Banks: A Field Experiment," *Political Research Quarterly* (forthcoming, 2004).

8. Alan S. Gerber, "Memo on the Effects of Partisan Direct Mail: Precinct-Level Experiments on Voter Turnout in a Congressional District," unpublished ms., Yale University, Institution for Social and Policy Studies, 2003.

9. Ricardo Ramírez, "Where No Party Has Gone Before . . . Non-Partisan Latino Voter Mobilization and Issues of Contactability," paper prepared for the Nation of Immigrants conference, University of California, Berkeley, Institute of Governmental Studies, May 2–3, 2003; Ricardo Ramírez, Alan S. Gerber, and Donald P. Green, "An Evaluation of NALEO's 2002 Voter Mobilization Campaign," unpublished ms., Yale University, Institution for Social and Policy Studies, 2003.

Appendix C

1. Samuel J. Eldersveld, "Experimental Propaganda Techniques and Voting Behavior," *American Political Science Review,* vol. 50 (March 1956), pp. 154–65; Roy E. Miller, David A. Bositis, and Denise L. Baer, "Stimulating Voter Turnout in a Primary: Field Experiment with a Precinct Committeeman," *International Political Science Review,* vol. 2, no. 4 (1981), pp. 445–60; William C. Adams and Dennis J. Smith, "Effects of Telephone Canvassing on Turnout and Preferences: A Field Experiment," *Public Opinion Quarterly,* vol. 44 (Autumn 1980), pp. 53–83.

2. Alan S. Gerber and Donald P. Green, "The Effects of Canvassing, Direct Mail, and Telephone Contact on Voter Turnout: A Field Experiment," *American Political Science Review,* vol. 94, no. 3 (2000), pp. 653–63. These figures differ from the published results due to post-publication corrections to the data.

3. Alan S. Gerber and Donald P. Green, "Do Phone Calls Increase Voter Turnout? A Field Experiment," *Public Opinion Quarterly,* vol. 65 (2001), pp. 75–85. Gerber and Green, "Effects of Canvassing, Direct Mail, and Telephone Contact." These figures differ from the published results due to post-publication corrections to the data.

4. The phone bank obviously was unable to contact those without working numbers.

5. Donald P. Green and Alan S. Gerber, "Getting Out the Youth Vote: Results

from Randomized Field Experiments," unpublished ms., Yale University, Institution for Social and Policy Studies, 2001. See also David W. Nickerson, "Phone Calls Can Increase Turnout: Evidence from Six Field Experiments," unpublished ms., Yale University, Institution for Social and Policy Studies, 2004.

6. David W. Nickerson, "Memo on the Effects of Phone Banking Campaigns during the 2001 Election," unpublished mss., Yale University, Institution for Social and Policy Studies, 2002.

7. Kevin Arceneaux, Alan S. Gerber, and Donald P. Green, "Two Large-Scale Field Experiments Using Phone Calls to Get Out the Vote: Comparing Experimental and Matching Methods," unpublished ms., Yale University, Institution for Social and Policy Studies, 2003.

8. Donald P. Green, Alan S. Gerber, and David W. Nickerson, "The Challenge of Bringing Voter Mobilization 'To Scale': An Evaluation of Youth Vote's 2002 Phone Banking Campaigns," unpublished ms., Yale University, Institution for Social and Policy Studies, 2003.

9. Ryan Friedrichs, "Mobilizing 18–35-Year-Old Voters: An Analysis of the Michigan Democratic Party's 2002 Youth Coordinated Campaign," unpublished thesis, Harvard University, John F. Kennedy School of Government, 2003; David W. Nickerson, "Memo Concerning Michigan Democratic Mobilization Experiment," unpublished ms., Yale University, Institution for Social and Policy Studies, 2003.

10. John E. McNulty, "Partisan Get-Out-the-Vote Drives and Turnout," paper presented at the annual meeting of the Midwest Political Science Association, Chicago, April 3–6, 2003.

11. Janelle Wong, "Getting Out the Vote among Asian Americans in Los Angeles County: A Field Experiment," paper presented at the annual meeting of the American Political Science Association, Philadelphia, August 28–31, 2003.

12. Donald P. Green, "Mobilizing African-American Voters Using Direct Mail and Commercial Phone Banks: A Field Experiment," *Political Research Quarterly* (forthcoming, 2004).

13. Ricardo Ramírez, "Where No Party Has Gone Before . . . Non-Partisan Latino Voter Mobilization and Issues of Contactability," paper prepared for presentation at the Nation of Immigrants conference, University of California, Berkeley, Institute of Governmental Studies, May 2–3, 2003; Ricardo Ramírez, Alan S. Gerber, and Donald P. Green, "An Evaluation of NALEO's 2002 Voter Mobilization Campaign," unpublished ms., Yale University, Institution for Social and Policy Studies, 2003.

Index